BEYOND THE PALE

BEYOND THE PALE
The Christian Political Fringe

DERRICK KNIGHT

CARAF

First published 1982 by Caraf Publications Ltd
Vicarage Flat, Carr Street, Leigh, Lancashire

Copyright © Derrick Knight 1982

British Library CIP Data
Knight, Derrick
    Beyond The Pale
      1. Christianity – South Africa
      2. Christianity and politics
      3. Fascism – South Africa
      I. Title
      320 9′68′06 BR1450

ISBN 0 907723 00 4

Printed by the Russell Press.

Cover design by Derek Bishton

Contents

Acknowledgements

The author and publishers gratefully acknowledge
permission to use copyright material from *National
Front* by Martin Walker, Fontana, and from *Fascists*
by Michael Billig, Academic Press Inc (London) Ltd.

Author's Note:

On legal advice a few paragraphs were omitted from this book as it
was about to go to press: this will explain the occasional small gaps
in the text.

Christians Against Racism and Fascism (CARAF) is pleased to publish this book as an essential part of its campaign against racism and fascism. The forces at work in promoting racism and fascism, including subtle methods of opposing those groups and individuals actively working for racial justice and harmony, are not always obvious. Yet it is clear that these forces, in one form or another, are capable of influencing many ordinary people through a well financed propaganda machine. 'Beyond the Pale' exposes both the forces and the machine.

CARAF is a membership organisation which seeks the support of Christians and others who are opposed to racism and fascism. It is a broad based campaign of all denominations, which supports and encourages Christians and Churches to work for a just and harmonious society with many races and cultures throughout Britain. CARAF believes that now is the time for Christians to stand with those who are suffering discrimination and injustice and, that those who practice racism and fascism are the greatest and most immediate threat to a harmonious community in Britain. Above all, CARAF sees opposition to racism and fascism as a central part of being a Christian. It is not a Christian optional extra, because racism and fascism challenge basic Christian values.

The following are CARAF's Statement of Aims:
* TO UNITE in the love of God, and our neighbours in the face of racist and Fascist ideology
* TO ACT as a broad ecumenical voice from the Christian church on issues of racism and Fascism
* TO PROMOTE an awareness among Christians of the dangers of fascism and the threats presented by Fascist organisations
* TO ASSIST the development of local Christian initiatives aimed at reducing the effectiveness of Fascist propaganda
* TO ENCOURAGE church leaders to oppose at national level the divisive policies and activities of organisations such as the National Front and the National Party
* TO CO-OPERATE with other initiatives aimed at promoting racial justice and opposing Fascism

Further information about CARAF and its work can be obtained from the Publications Officer, CARAF, Vicarage Flat, Carr Street, Leigh, Lancashire.

David Jennings
Chairperson, CARAF.

August 1981

Preface

In 1977, a booklet called *The Fraudulent Gospel* was published. It was written by Bernard Smith, a religious polemicist, one-time enthusiastic member of the Monday Club and National Front sympathizer. In it he attacked the World Council of Churches and Christian ecumenism in all its manifestations. He also argued against what he saw as 'money for terrorists' — the special grants made to liberation movements in southern Africa through the Special Fund of the Programme to Combat Racism of the World Council of Churches. The booklet was disordered and the language so extreme that it deserved to be ignored. But this did not happen; talk about it as a serious manifestation of Christian concern seemed to grow and spread. The booklet, and the organizations and interests which publicized it, appeared to be only an element in a much wider spectrum of religious and political fringe activity. This activity was not limited to Britain; it had its parallels in other countries.

There is nothing new about the presence of extremist political and religious sects or groups in Britain. Indeed the British pride themselves on their tolerance. Such groups usually have small followings, in some cases limited to one or two individuals with a particular bee in their bonnets. In the past, these groups as a general rule have been as implacably opposed to each other as to their target enemy, with the more bizarre religious groups forming a kind of sad, dotty fringe. However, in the last few years a spirit of co-operation seems to have come upon many of them. Was it chance, opportunism or a planned strategy? The cacophony of conflicting issues and phobias usually heard from the fringe suddenly changed into a number of common themes which were orchestrated into a kind of ensemble. The repertoire was small but familiar. The first theme was the Marxist threat to white Western civilization. The second was the danger of multi-racialism. The third was the horror of the terrorist threat to southern Africa, helped by the British churches. The fourth was that British churches were run by sub-versives, the Archbishop of Canterbury being a Soviet agent and all the bishops communists, and behind them lay the Marxist World Council of Churches run by the KGB. Anyone familiar with the propaganda themes of the South African Government knew all of these as old favourites.

Suspicions about a South African connection were confirmed when the Muldergate information scandal broke. There was no doubt that the South Africans were trying to 'manage' the far right, and the far right, recognising a certain identity of interest, was playing along, flattered by the new sense of status it gave and by the resources offered for propagating controversial views.

The South African Department of Information's secret projects list (which has only been partly revealed) included initiatives aimed at discrediting the authority of the major Protestant Church denominations, in Britain and elsewhere, by exploiting the fears and doubts of their members. By doing so it was hoped to neutralize the stubborn Christian opposition to the racist policies of the Republic of South Africa; to defuse the campaign of disinvestment launched by many church bodies; to draw attention away from South Africa's dismal record on human rights; and to stop worldwide support for the South African Council of Churches — almost the last independent centre of Christian witness against apartheid inside South Africa itself. The official South African view has always been that the 'conscience' of virtually all churches outside South Africa is misguided and part of that great world communist conspiracy to overwhelm the last true bastion of the 'free world'. Put in its simplest terms, the object of the South African Information Department was to discredit the growing mission of the world churches — to combat the evils of racism and to seek social justice for the poor and the oppressed — as un-Christian, and to deny the churches' right to engage in any 'political' activity.

One can readily understand why a costly South African initiative should be mounted to attempt to find political allies or to change public opinion. It is perhaps less obvious why there should be a determined campaign against the churches, whose influence is considerable but whose membership is only a small fraction of the population of their countries. The reason has to be that the country which has 'God on its side' finds it unbearable that all the major denominations and all the significant leadership of the world's churches are against it. This opposition is symbolized by the World Council of Churches. So no effort has been spared to discredit the Christian opponents of apartheid. They have been attacked through their national church councils, through their charities such as Christian Aid, by smear tactics against their leaders or against particular denominations, and by attempting to breach the fellowship of the churches in the World Council of Churches.

The timing for such attacks has been well thought out. The late 1970s was a period when many people of moderate political and social opinions were bored with traditional issues; sceptical about the value of mainstream politics; uneasy about the economic crisis and the threat of worldwide recession, unemployment, immigration, violence; shaken out of their faith in fundamental values; and in short, worried about the future and nostalgic for a way of life which may be passing forever. A mood that still prevails.

It is such fears and tensions that the National Front and similar groups of a fascist character have tried to exploit and some Christians undoubtedly feel attracted to them and their ideas. The National Front implacably attacks the social gospel of the churches.

It is, however, mainly South African cash, South African agents and South African information that have been used to discredit the World Council of Churches, the British Council of Churches, the various anti-apartheid groups, the Liberal Party of Great Britain, and similar groups in the major industrial countries of Europe and North America and the 'white' Commonwealth countries of Australia and New Zealand.

The object of this book is to provide an overview of current right-wing groupings, their connections, their strategies, their activities. These groups, and the individuals who run them, are worth listing: this helps the process of demystification. Very often a list of grandiose-sounding organizations are the facets of just one individual who can use these bogus organizations as leverage on behalf of a non-existent pressure group.

In the main these are a small, untypical, unrepresentative number of slightly dotty clergy and their friends, some of whom have been around for a long time and whose bizarre notions have hitherto found no wide support. They certainly represent a dangerous element, but it is the South African connection which makes them a serious threat. It is now a matter of public interest that all such activities, which are basically anti-democratic and aimed at the heart of our society, should be exposed.

I have spoken to many people and corresponded with many groups and organizations in the United Kingdom and overseas

11

and I am grateful for all the help and encouragement they have given me and the generous way they have been prepared to share the fruits of their expertise and research. I acknowledge my debt to them all. Special thanks to Roger Williamson, who provided the text on West Germany, and to Barbara Rogers, whose special knowledge of the United States situation was generously made available to the author.

List of Initials of Organisations Mentioned in the Text

AAM	Anti-Apartheid Movement
BCC	British Council of Churches
BOSS	Bureau of State Security (South Africa)
CAC	Christian Affirmation Campaign
CCBP	Confederation of Church and Business People (Canada)
C-Far	Citizens for Foreign Aid Reform (Canada)
CIA	Central Intelligence Agency of the US
CLSA	Christian League of Southern Africa
CPD	Committee on the Present Danger
DOI	Department of Information of South Africa
EKD	Evangelische Kirche in Deutschland
FARI	Foreign Affairs Research Institute
FEMACE	Federation of Mexican Anti-Communists
FWF	Forum World Features
ICCC	International Council of Christian Churches (USA)
ICCR	Interfaith Center for Corporate Responsibility
ICN	International Christian Network
ISC	Institute for the Study of Conflict
ISSA	Information Service of South Africa
NAF	National Association for Freedom (now the Freedom Association)
NCCC	National Council of the Churches of Christ (USA)
NF	National Front
NGK	Nederlands Gereformeerde Kerk
NSIC	National Strategy Information Centre
PCR	Programme to Combat Racism
SACC	South African Council of Churches
TFG	The Fraudulent Gospel
WCC	World Council of Churches
WACL	World Anti-Communist League

Introduction

In the early 1970s a small group of Christians — some two dozen or so — all disenchanted with the major church denominations and calling themselves the Christian Affirmation Campaign (CAC), began a sustained crusade in Britain against what they saw as the politicization of Christianity through its ecumenical organizations — the British Council of Churches and its support of the World Council of Churches. The CAC affirmed that it was itself apolitical and only concerned with helping people return to traditional forms of Christianity. But the CAC has a number of connections with right-wing political groups which shed a dubious light on the Christian motives it proclaims. Its secretary Bernard Smith, a teacher, has a long history of right-wing political and religious agitation. He is a veteran pamphleteer and letter-writer to the press. His themes are usually 'politics and the church', the 'Anglican sell-out to communism', 'opposition to immigration', and 'money to terrorists'.[1]

One of Smith's closest allies is Donald Martin of the British League of Rights and other such bodies. With the Dowager Lady Jane Birdwood, Martin is joint-secretary of the British Chapter of the World Anti-Communist League (WACL) which ranks President Stroessner of Paraguay and until lately, General Somoza of Nicaragua, amongst its most important patrons and heroes. Martin returned to Britain in 1970 from Australia where he had been closely associated with Eric Butler, a man regarded as a mentor by many who are considered to be active racists and anti-semites. He is also the leader of the Australian League of Rights. A network of newsletters and publications exists in which the views of these people are spread through a variety of innocent-sounding societies and organizations.[2] WACL has close connections with violent and neo-Nazi groups around the world[3] and with the National Front, Britain's largest right-wing party which attempts to disguise its bitter racialism and anti-semitism behind a patriotic label. Right-wing parties such as the National Front and the British Movement have their own

15

reasons for attacking the churches, although they pose as Christians defending white Christian civilization.

In *The Fraudulent Gospel* Bernard Smith attacked vigorously the churches' support of 'money for terrorists', by which he meant the special grants given for humanitarian purposes to liberation movements in southern Africa as part of the World Council of Churches Programme to Combat Racism. The arguments developed were thinly supported and the language was hysterical. Nevertheless, the booklet was republished in South Africa[4] and circulated mainly through mail-order booksellers[5] specializing in Nazi and similar cult literature with a strong racist or anti-semitic bias. It was clear that *TFG* (as it is known) was being pushed, with the aid of resources beyond those of the small political and religious groups which were immediately to hand.

A South African connection was suspected before the Department of Information scandal was uncovered and this was confirmed as the story of slush funds supporting secret projects around the world became known.

A little publicized part of the former South African Department of Information's propaganda programme to buy political influence and 'manage' the media around the world was the programme of secret projects aimed at church membership and Christian organizations. One of the targets in Britain was Christian Aid for allegedly supporting 'terrorism' in southern Africa; but the entire leadership of the British churches was accused of surrendering to 'modernism', a phrase loosely used to designate all who attempt to interpret the Bible and religion along evolutionary or progressive lines, and used as a 'smear' to criticize any move to change the form of worship or the texts used in it. A campaign was mounted within the Church of England to try and stop the annual grants approved at General Synod to the World Council of Churches.

The aim of the Department of Information programme was fourfold: first to neutralize the stubborn and vocal opposition to apartheid; second to halt disinvestment campaigns in Europe and America in which the churches were often deeply involved; third to discredit the World Council of Churches which was supporting anti-apartheid movements and co-ordinating moral pressure against South Africa's racist policies; fourth to destroy the South African Council of Churches, which was almost the last important centre of independent Christian witness against apartheid within South Africa, by attempting to cut off its worldwide support. Hundreds of thousands of pounds were allocated to this international campaign.

A Christian pressure group called The Christian League of Southern Africa, which had its HQ in Pretoria, had long been suspected by many journalists and church leaders of being involved in the 'grand design' of propaganda projects mounted by the DOI's Executive Secretary Dr Eschel Rhoodie during the period from 1975 to 1978. It was directed by the Rev Fred Shaw, a Methodist minister who had rebelled against the main body of the Methodist Church in South Africa.

The growth of the Christian League parallels the unfolding of the DOI's more ambitious and costly projects to influence world opinion. Throughout the period of investigation into the information scandal by the press and by legal commissions, the director of the Christian League denied any connection with the DOI. But during the summer of 1979 Dr Eschel Rhoodie,[6] having escaped from South Africa, gave documents and a lengthy interview to an old friend, now editor of the Dutch magazine *Elseviers*. In an account of the many projects his department initiated, Rhoodie detailed the funding of the Christian League as Project G-11c, codename Bernard.

The South African press had been making its own investigations. At an earlier stage John Matisonn, the political correspondent of the Johannesburg *Sunday Express*,[7] had linked the Christian League with the DOI. He disclosed that the Rev Fred Shaw kept an unauthorized bank account in the United States, and that there were strong links between Shaw's organization and various well-known DOI fronts. Shaw brought a legal complaint against Matisonn. The case went to appeal and is still pending at the time of writing. In November 1979, however, Pik Botha, South Africa's foreign minister, asked by the Afrikaans newspaper *Die Transvaler* to comment on criticisms of the authorities handling the Matisonn case, revealed that the League had received taxpayers money in secret. He said: 'It is not clear to me how the financial support which was given by the former Department of Information to the Christian League of Southern Africa has any connection with the case.'[8]

In May 1980 the published evidence of the Erasmus Commission, the official legal enquiry into the South African Information Department scandal, finally confirmed that the Christian League was an Information Department front.[9]

In the meantime the Methodist Church of South Africa had carried out its own investigation of the CLSA and produced a highly critical report which recommended that Methodists should have nothing to do with the CLSA or its directors.

The Christian League had been expanding its activities in Britain since 1976. Copies of its English newspaper *Encounter*, printed in South Africa, were flown to Schipol Airport in Holland and mailed free to a wide list of clergymen and church leaders in Britain. It was also distributed in North America. Its editorial policy unfailingly followed the South African Nationalist Government policy.

A series of pamphlets of a generally scurrilous nature, attacking the churches for supporting the WCC, for 'sharing the responsibility for the deaths of missionaries' and for supporting the black liberation movements in southern Africa, were regularly circulated by hand around London and some other city centres, posted from the League's London office, or added to the regular mailings of friendly organizations. In 1979, and again in 1980, a pamphlet attacking Christian Aid was circulated in the weeks prior to that charity's major fund-raising week. It directly accused Christian Aid of 'helping terrorists' by making gifts to the ZAPU and ZANU organizations in Rhodesia (now the government of independent Zimbabwe) and used an atrocity photograph to increase its impact.

The leading members of the Christian League have been regular participants in the meetings of the Christian Affirmation Campaign and their material regularly mailed by CAC together with its own. Bernard Smith contributes articles to *Encounter* and provides research on Christian activities in Britain of interest to the South Africans in the Christian League. Smith's booklet *TFG* is published in South Africa by Valiant Publishers, which was revealed as a DOI front. The booklet's English publisher Geoffrey Stewart-Smith has long-standing associations with causes which include para-military organizations. He also has close connections with South African government officials.[10]

A loose network of traditional Christians in Europe in the early 1970s were searching for some kind of co-ordinated movement around which the standard of opposition to 'modernism' could be raised. The spiritual pole on which this standard was raised became known as the Berlin Declaration on Ecumenism. A loose fellowship of these 'confessing' Christians existed through 1976 and up to 1978. Its members shared newsletters, published each other's articles and sought opportunities to promote themselves in the media.

The catalyst which brought these scattered people and ideas together was the Christian League. In the mid-1970s it was expanded, as we now know, with help from the South African Government. It had offices throughout South Africa and a spacious HQ in Pretoria with a full-time staff of ten. In addition to *Encounter*, it published in German *Vox Africana*, aimed at German Protestant churchmen. The League alone had the organization, the address lists, the travelling budget, the financial resources and the ambition, to carry the Nationalist 'Christian' message into the hostile world. However, it needed a theological argument which could be defended on general principles and not linked solely to South Africa. It also needed a single issue which could unite ordinary Christians all over the world. The Berlin Declaration, with its call to traditional Christianity, provided the first. The second was the spectre of terrorism, linked with a warning of how communism was spreading throughout Africa and indeed putting the whole Christian world at peril. We are in the front line now trying to stem the return of barbarism, it will be your turn next, was the message.

The anti-communist issue also unlocked the doors of a whole range of conservative evangelical groups in different parts of the world and brought the League into close affinity with a wide spectrum of right-wing radicals. The International Christian Network, the outcome of these negotiations, was launched in London in the summer of 1978. The main sponsors were the Christian League of Southern Africa, the Rhodesia Christian Group — its affiliate — and the Christian Affirmation Campaign.

These connections have enabled the Christian League to achieve the co-operation of a wide range of large and small pressure groups in promoting the views of white South Africa. A Christian underworld of a sort has probably always existed and been ignored. The Christian League and its allies have dragged much of this underworld into the open and put it to work. What is true of the style of the British connection has its parallels in North America, West Germany, Holland and in the so-called white Commonwealth contries — Australia and New Zealand. All the principal leaders and active protagonists view contemporary events as in the grip of a giant conspiracy. History itself, they think, is a conspiracy, set in motion by demonic forces of almost transcendant power and the usual methods of political give-and-take will not defeat it. What is needed is an all-out crusade. The governing Nationalist Party of South Africa shares this view. The techniques of subversion used to persuade the rest of us require permanent vigilance and questioning about the complex issues which increasingly dominate our lives.

References

1. See for instance 'Primate's Selective Indignation against SA' in *Encounter* newspaper, April 1978; letters on 9 and 20 March 1979 in the *Daily Telegraph;* pamphlet *Christian Aid: The Politics of Charity* of the Christian Affirmation Campaign.

2. The Housewives' League; Safeguard Britain Campaign; The British League for European Freedom, etc.

3. See full description in Chapter 2.

4. By Valiant Publishers, revealed in 1978 as a front of the defunct Department of Information.

5. See Appendix on page 184.

6. Rhoodie was evenutally extradited from France, stood trial in South Africa on seven counts of fraud, was found guilty on five and sentenced to six years imprisonment. He was released on appeal in October 1979. A British journalist who went looking for him in April 1980 found he was on a hiking holiday. On 29 September 1980, the Appeal Court in Bloemfontein set aside the fraud conviction and six-year jail sentence on Dr Rhoodie. The court said that his evidence could, in the salient aspects at least, be possibly true. Later his property, his assets and his passport were returned to him. He announced that he was writing a book which would blow the lid off all the secret projects he promoted while at the former Department of Information.

7. *Sunday Express*, 3 December 1978.

8. *Die Transvaler*, 29 November 1979.

9. *Rand Daily Mail*, 16 May 1980 etc.

10. See 'Geoffrey Stewart-Smith, Belper's "secret" Tory MP', from Parliamentary Profiles, 3/4 Palace Chambers, Bridge Street, London, SW1. Stewart-Smith's FARI arranged visits of MPs and others to South Africa for the South African Foreign Affairs Association and hosted South African military intelligence and other figures at the Brighton Conference in July 1978. People's News Service 17 May 1979 alleges FARI was set up by the South Africans in 1974 and subsidized at a rate of £85,000 a year.

1. The Company They Keep

In order to find out more about the nature of an organization, an early step is usually to examine the links between it and other related organizations, to observe the people moving between them and to record and analyze what they have to say in public and in private about their aims and objectives. It is then possible to build up a coherent picture of these groups. It follows that the connection and common objectives of the members of the Christian Affirmation Campaign (CAC), the Christian League of Southern Africa (CLSA), the Rhodesia Christian Group (RCG), and the umbrella organization of the International Christian Network (ICN), plus a variety of other religious and political entities in Britain and overseas, can be looked at in this way and their common aims and objectives deduced exactly as if they were part of some underground movement.

It appears that in some senses these organizations are just that, having an overt and very public role, but at the same time an evolving covert role.

The Christian Affirmation Campaign

On 9 June 1979, the CAC held one of its occasional conferences in central London. The conference was advertised in the classified columns of selected church publications, but the main invitations went out through the mailings of related organizations. The location was 31 Green Street, the London base of CHIPS — the Christian International Peace Service — a charity offering rooms 'for Christian and charitable use'. Up the dark oak staircase came about 40 white people to hear a panel of speakers, lined up in a row facing the grand piano in the first-floor front sitting-room. The small library downstairs became a useful bookshop.

The press was not invited, but not specifically barred either. However, the photographer sent by *Searchlight*, the British anti-fascist magazine, was refused admittance. CAC was suspicious of the national papers which in the main had refused to take the group seriously. In any case, most of the speakers and several guests controlled their own newsletters and mailing lists to their own faithful flocks. No reporters tried to cover the event, but a freelance photographer was permitted to record the occasion and from his pictures and the CAC's own hand-outs, it has been possible to identify, not just the main speakers, but also many of the other participants, whose organizations are well known, and the origin of much of the literature being offered on the two bookstalls.

Even an incomplete list of those who attended the conference and what they represent, provides a guide to the interests and concerns of the CAC.

Rather than risk a hostile press, the CAC put out its own release after the meeting which emphasized the 'crowded' room and the simple anti-World Council of Churches message of the German guest speaker Dr Peter Beyerhaus. The Secretary of the CAC is Bernard Smith, a teacher and freelance journalist who formed the CAC in 1974 and runs it from his home in Gidea Park, Romford. Its overt aims are to promote 'true Christianity', maintain the traditional Christian ethic, and warn innocent Christians of the danger of association with such bodies as the World Council of Churches. Smith is an Erastian Anglican, politically well to the right.

The Rev Fred Shaw, the Chairman of the CLSA, had flown in from Pretoria to support his London representative Graeham Blainey and former colleague the Rev David Kingdon at this meeting. The objectives of the League are to ward off a black takeover in southern Africa, and to oppose 'politics' in the Church. It campaigns against the work of the South African Council of Churches, against the World Council of Churches, and more recently against Christian Aid in the United Kingdom. For these objectives there has apparently been substantial financial backing. A fuller discussion of the operations of the League is contained in Chapter 4.

At the time of the conference the Rev David Kingdon was the first secretary of the International Christian Network, which has offices at 53 Victoria Street, Westminster. David Kingdon is a Baptist whose personal theological beliefs have taken him out of the Baptist Union. He emigrated to South Africa in 1974 to become a minister in Pretoria, where his kind of Calvinism was in tune with that of the Dutch Reformed Church. He became a member of the staff of the CLSA and returned to Britain in the autumn of 1978.

Since that time he has spoken for the Christian League, and opened the London office of the International Christian Network with which the CLSA is affiliated, and with which it shares offices.*

Graeham Blainey, the CLSA London representative, also spoke at the meeting. Little is known about Blainey's background, but he lived for a time in South Africa where he was recruited by the CLSA. In Britain he has been an active representative, publishing and personally distributing leaflets attacking sanctions against Rhodesia, disinvestment in South Africa, the United Nations, the British Government, but above all the World Council of Churches and the British churches which support it.

Another speaker was Donald Martin, who also helped to chair the meeting and ran a bookstall on behalf of his British League of Rights. Donald Martin returned to Britain in 1970 from Australia where he had been closely associated with Eric Butler, a man considered a mentor by active racists and anti-semites throughout the English-speaking world and leader of the Australian League of Rights. Since his return to Britain Martin has founded the British League of Rights. He publishes a fortnightly newsletter called *On Target*[1] which is anti-Common Market, opposes immigration, and is anti-communist. Martin is also co-chairman, with the Dowager Lady Birdwood, of the British Chapter of the World Anti-Communist League (WACL), which has close connections with neo-Nazis and with the National Front. An old friend of Bernard Smith, Martin has been connected with CAC since its beginnings. He was a speaker at an earlier CAC conference held at Uckfield.**

Hamish Fraser, a Scottish Catholic convert who was billed as 'a former Marxist and political commissar in the Spanish Civil War', spoke on 'the menace of Christian Marxism'. His is a voice from the distant past, once notorious in church press circles for the virulence and persistence of his letter-writing campaigns.

Also on the speakers' panel was the intellectual lynch-pin of the International Christian Network, its chairman Dr Peter Beyerhaus from West Germany, billed as Director of the Institute of Missiology and Ecumenical Theology of Tübingen University. Beyerhaus, a one-time missionary in South Africa and a severe critic of the World Council of Churches, is repelled by mainstream theology which is more and more concerned with social issues, especially with the liberation of the oppressed.

*Since then Kingdon resigned from ICN and accepted a Baptist pastorate in a village just beyond Cardigan in Wales.

**He was guest speaker at the CAC conference at Battle in 1981; his subject "The Powers of Darkness and the Christian Answer".

He sees a sinister world conspiracy in the ecumenical movement which is, in his view, controlled by atheistic Marxists. It is his belief that the churches should return to biblical religion. The Network purports to be a fellowship of those with similar views.

Those who gave vocal support from the floor of the meeting included two young representatives of the Unification Church, known in this country as the 'Moonies', a South Korean sect which has been investigated by the Faith and Order Commission of the National Council of Churches in the United States, which concluded that its claims to Christian identity cannot be recognized.

There were also two representatives of the Freedom Association, formerly the National Association for Freedom. Its former director, John Gouriet, became well known to the general public through his support of George Ward in the Grunwick dispute and his attempt to stop a postal workers' boycott of South Africa. He is a CAC supporter and spoke at a previous conference. The Freedom Association's paper *The Free Nation* has published an attack on Christian Aid by Rachel Tingle, whose husband Philip van de Elst spoke at the CAC's Uckfield conference in 1978. Also in the audience was Kenneth McKilliam, a founder member of the National Front and still very active. He is a supporter of the British Israelite Movement and among his favourite targets are Freemasonary and the 'Financial-Zionist-Communist International Conspiracy' to destroy Britain. He is also one of a close circle of friends and colleagues of Mary Stanton, whose Free Society and National Assembly has a small but evolving role in extreme right-wing politics. McKilliam's virulent racist pamphlets *Revealing Anti-Christ* and *Our Nation is Being Destroyed* were being offered for sale during the conference.

David Watson, another participant, is an ex-teacher who enjoyed brief notoriety in the press when he was instructed to stop teaching what he saw as the literal truth of the Biblical Creation, condemning Darwinian theories as lies. His booklets *The Great Brain Robbery: Creation or Evolution* and *Myths and Miracles* are being promoted by the CAC.* Finally, there was Philip Vickers, the director of Aid to the Church in Need (ACN),[2] many of whose booklets were on sale.

ACN is a well-established Roman Catholic charity working principally with refugees and Christians in communist countries of Eastern Europe. Vickers is also on the board of directors of

---

* The CAC also promote The Biblical Creation Society, a body founded in 1976 to unite Christians opposed to the theory of evolution.

Keston College for the study of religion and communism,[3] a respected research organization which monitors and issues briefings on the state of religious communities in the Soviet Union and Eastern European socialist countries.

A regular member of such meetings who was unable to attend was Father Arthur Lewis,[4] the Anglican missionary and former senator in Ian Smith's Parliament who heads the Rhodesia Christian Group. In October 1978 he was banned from returning to this country by the Foreign Office. At this CAC conference he was represented by the Rev Maurice Cartledge, a Methodist minister from the Midlands who has done his best through the years to act as an echo-chamber for his distant colleagues.

The CAC meeting has been described rather fully, not because anything of particular importance was said or done, but because it was fairly typical of such occasions in previous years. It produced the same sort of support from the same or similar organizations. Since 1974, when the CAC was formed, it has, it would appear from the attendance at advertised meetings, gained no general public support. It relies on the company and fellowship of organizations of broadly similar viewpoint. Nevertheless, the views it expresses have been widely disseminated.

References

1. *On Target* is published by Intelligence Publications (UK), The Old Priory, Priory Walk, Sudbury, Suffolk. This is also the address of Bloomfield Books, The British Housewives' League and other Donald Martin interests.

2. Aid to the Church in Need was founded as Iron Curtain Church Relief in 1947 by Father Werenfried von Straaten. British headquarters are at 3–5 North Street, Chichester, West Sussex.

3. Keston College, Keston, Kent. Its headquarters are an old converted school in the Kent village of Keston from which it takes its name. Keston College is a charity, funded mainly by church groups in Holland, Germany and Scandinavia and to a lesser degree by local churches and individuals in Britain.

4. Following the birth of Zimbabwe, Father Lewis moved to Pretoria and has issued his occasional newsletters from South Africa.

2. '. . . Where Angels Fear to Tread'

Anyone curious about the Christian Affirmation Campaign who writes to Bernard Smith, its secretary, or to Mary Hopson, its publicity organizer, will get a personal and friendly reply and an envelope full of leaflets, newsletters and handouts. These will explain the main principles of the campaign and the issues which concern it. There will also be papers from a variety of other groups and causes with which the CAC has an affinity.

A correspondent who wrote asking for information in January 1979 received the CAC broadsheet, a flyer offering *The Fraudulent Gospel*, a photostat article by Bernard Smith attacking the churches for not condemning the World Council of Churches for 'supporting terrorism', a pamphlet called *Three Reasons Why Christians Cannot Support the WCC*, a copy of *Encounter*, the newspaper produced by the Christian League of Southern Africa, and a newsletter by Father Arthur Lewis of the Rhodesia Christian Group.

Another mailing in 1979 contained, in addition to a news-letter, a personal appeal from the London Secretary of the Christian League of Southern Africa 'to do everything possible to help Rhodesia overcome the satanic forces which are now close to engulfing her!', a flyer for a Caxton Hall meeting on Rhodesia to be addressed by Patrick Wall MP, John Gouriet of the Freedom Association and Bernard Smith, primarily on the subject of the Foreign Office ban on Father Lewis, and a photo-stat advertisement in the Freedom Association newspaper by the CLSA headed 'SAVE RHODESIA, Rhodesia's enemy is Britain's Enemy'.

Other literature which has been circulated by the CAC includes sample leaflets by the Christian Mission to the Com-munist World; back issues of *East-West Digest*, a magazine produced by Geoffrey Stewart-Smith's Foreign Affairs Publish-ing Company whose main theme is the communist threat to white Western civilization; sample copies of *Housewives Today* and *On Target*, both newsletters of a strong anti-immigration hue, written and distributed by Donald Martin of the British

League of Rights, and copies of the *National Layman's Digest*, a publication of the Church League of America (a research centre to document radical movements in politics and the church in the United States).

The CAC is not only a religious pressure group with a 'traditionalist' line — it is a political group with many right-wing links and interests. As a body laying down the principle that Christianity should be separated from politics, it is itself deeply engaged in political controversy and political actions.

Bernard Smith, Founder of CAC

In its public relations, the CAC is helpful and friendly. Correspondence is handwritten and chatty, membership is free and 'quite informal'. In appearance, Bernard Smith — like some latter-day Old Testament prophet with his high dome, bald crown and aureole of artfully tended grey whiskers and beard — is an unlikely crusader to be fulminating against the World Council of Churches, the English bishops, Christian Aid and many other targets from the quiet backwaters of a Romford suburb. During the day he teaches in a local mixed junior school, but in the evening and in all his spare time he lectures and admonishes a much wider audience through his pen.

Smith is not well known to the general public, but the religious press know him and so do the editors of some right-wing journals. In 1977 an article of his attacking Christian Aid was published in *Spearhead*, the magazine of the National Front owned by John Tyndall. Smith's brand of polemic is good provocative copy and editors are always looking for issues to encourage people to engage in controversy. He has one or two main targets[1] which he never tires of, but some others include:

the Anglican Church
'has traded moral leadership for a mess of political pottage'

women and ordination
'It is a self-evident fact that the Christian Church abhors priestesses, it . . . should, in my view, go on doing so.'

evolution
'It's a myth, a fantasy, and offends against common sense . . . It has changed us from a Christian to a pagan nation . . .'

27

human rights
'Since the Left has insinuated itself into all the human rights movements, the whole fabric of deceit is smeared over with the odious grease of "justice" and "compassion".'

charity
'appeals that always reduce Christians to a mindless state of bovine goodwill'

abortion
'plain evil'

intellectuals
'They have managed by their sneers to kill patriotism in this country and they have done their best to make Christianity an embarrassment to Christians.'

Smith is a writer with a self-confessed interest in the overlap between religion and politics, but he is not a linesman, he is a player. *The Crooked Conscience*, written in 1972 for the Monday Club, the right-wing Conservative ginger group, emerged out of the same ferment in that Tory group which produced the infamous pamphlet by G K Young called *Who Goes Home?* (about the repatriation of coloured immigrants) and which threatened a National Front takeover of the Club. Smith was a Monday Club member at that time. His pamphlet, subtitled *Are the churches politically bent?* answers the question in the affirmative, contrasting the concern of the western churches with apartheid in South Africa with, in his view, the lack of a similar concern for Christians behind the Iron Curtain. He saw this as a deliberately political bias in allegedly moral causes and as part of a worldwide subversion of the churches by Marxist atheism. He named the Baptist World Alliance, the British (sic) Missionary Society, the International Commission of Jurists, the United Nations Commission on Human Rights, Canon Collins, Bishop Sansbury, Dr Carson Blake, the Rev Paul Oestreicher and the World Council of Churches as part of this conspiracy, what he calls elsewhere a 'spiritual fifth column'. He returned to the same themes in *The Fraudulent Gospel*, which was published in 1977.

The Fraudulent Gospel — Another Kind of 'Little Red Book'

The Fraudulent Gospel, subtitled *Politics and the World Council of Churches*, is a slim paperback. The cover photograph on the first edition is of black Rhodesians killed in the civil war and the theme of the booklet is revealed by the explanation which states: 'cover photograph: 27 Black Rhodesians *massacred by WCC-financed terrorists* (our italics) in Eastern Rhodesia in December 1976.' The photo originates from *The Citizen*, the government-sponsored English-speaking newspaper in South Africa.

The blurb for the first edition described it as 'a searing critique of the anti-Christian views and actions of the World Council of Churches'. The blurb to the second edition emphasizes Smith's allegation that Christian churchgoers in Britain are unwittingly giving financial assistance to communist-backed terrorist organizations in Africa.

Apart from a revamped introduction and a couple of extended chapters, the second edition is identical to the first. There are no corrections of fact, or amendments to meet changing situations, although the booklet has been completely reset by the printer.

Once more, according to the publishers, the main theme of the booklet is the World Council of Churches' 'infatuation with revolutionary politics'. The WCC's policies are 'consistently anti-Western and pro-Soviet'. The WCC, Smith writes, has given Marxist politics a Christian justification, 'by popularizing the ideas of "secular ecumenism" '. The WCC's final goals are, he says, 'a unified humanity and a collectivist world state'.

In his chapter on 'The WCC and African Terrorists', Smith is deeply critical of the controversial Programme to Combat Racism and concludes that liberation movements cannot reasonably be expected to get church support. Another chapter on 'Education for Liberation' accuses the WCC of taking a 'frankly Marxist' attitude. In other chapters on Black Power in Britain, human rights in the Soviet Union, Soviet Jews, North American Indians, the Vietnam war, South Korea and the missionary field, Smith lays out his arguments about the bogus theology of the WCC and concludes that 'this *fraudulent theology* is sufficient proof that the WCC is anti-Christ'.

TFG was priced at £1 in 1977. The revised edition issued in August 1979 was still offered at £1, despite soaring costs and a new layout. This seemed a curious situation.

In the UK *TFG* is published by the Foreign Affairs Publishing Co Ltd, Church House, Petersham, Richmond, which is owned by Geoffrey Stewart-Smith. The address is also his home. No figures are available either for the costs of the book or for sales, but it is reasonable to suppose that ordinary sales, by which is meant unsupported across-the-counter sales by the publisher, would be on the low side. The subject matter is specialized, Christian Affirmation Campaign has only a small body of supporters, and it is not an obvious choice for profitable speculation. But the Foreign Affairs Publishing Co does not appear to work like an ordinary publisher. It published *East-West Digest*, a monthly review (now temporarily suspended) which was distributed to all MPs, most peers and some other opinion-formers free of charge, and therefore presumably heavily subsidized. *East-West Digest* is a compilation of anti-communist features, documenting the alleged activities of the Russian world conspiracy and the radical left in Britain, with which it is supposed to have links. Foreign Affairs Publishing produce other books on similar themes such as *Inside the KGB*, an exposé by an officer of the Third Directorate, Aleksei Myagkov; *The Communist Challenge* by Ian Grieg; *The Destruction of Loyalty* – an examination of the threat of propaganda and subversion against the armed forces of the west – by Anthony Burton. Some of these books are marketed at a price which makes no sense in commercial terms. R W Johnson, in a review in the *New Statesman* 6 January 1978, had this to say about Grieg's book *The Communist Challenge*:

> 'I rang the publisher and asked how one could bring out a hard-cover book in these days for £3. Well, I was told, it was a strictly commercial operation, but, yes, the book was probably under-priced – perhaps it should have been £4. I rang another publisher who hooted with laughter and insisted that a break-even price could not be lower than £8. Either there was a hidden subsidy of 100 per cent plus, he suggested, or the book would have to be bulk-bought and distributed virtually free by some embassy or propaganda service . . .'

Geoffrey Stewart-Smith had occasional publishing contracts with Valiant Publishers in South Africa and *The Fraudulent Gospel* and the Grieg book were published by Valiant for South Africa. At a news conference in Johannesburg reported in the *Guardian* on 25 November 1978 Mr Metrowich, the managing director of Valiant, disclosed that he was paid a salary by the government and admitted that his publishing company and its subsidiaries received government money.*

As a further stage in the Muldergate enquiry was reached, it was revealed in South Africa that Valiant publishers and its subsidiaries were the publishing arm of another front organization, the South

---

* The chairman of the South Africa Freedom Foundation was Mr 'Red' Metrowich. He had formerly been a writer for the virulent SABC programme "Current Affairs". He then joined the Africa Institute – a government sponsored foundation where his pre-occupation with 'communism in Africa' was reinforced. He then launched Valiant after a meeting with Dr Eschel Rhoodie. Valiant published mainly anti-communist literature.

Africa Freedom Foundation, which has since been closed in the wake of the defunct Department of Information exposure.

In the United States, *TFG* is published by the Church League of America (see Chapter 7) which, according to its own blurb, is the largest private research organization and information centre on the operations of the Communist Party and the New Left movement in the entire United States. The League is run by Edgar Bundy, a former Air Force intelligence officer, a friend of the Rev Fred Shaw (chairman of the CLSA) and listed as one of the sponsors of the CLSA North American speakers' tour in the autumn of 1978.

How TFG and Similar Literature is Distributed

You are unlikely to find *TFG* in Charing Cross Road booksellers or high street bookshops anywhere. It is basically a mail-order item offered through the CAC and similar groups and by specialist book catalogues which come through the post.

One example is the Pro Fide Book Service, recently renamed St Duthac's Book Service. It appeals mainly to 'traditionalist' Catholics, but it offers TFG too. The attraction of such catalogues for propagandists is that they can, if they so wish, host racist material with slight risk of prosecution. The Historical Review Press in Brighton promotes a list of hard-core anti-semitic and fascist tracts, including the notorious *Did Six Million Really Die?* by Richard Harwood, alias Richard Verrall, one of the theorists of the National Front.* Bloomfield Books, in Sudbury, Suffolk, which also offers such catalogues, is the pamphlet and book outlet for Donald Martin's various activities, including *On Target* and the British League of Rights.

In 1975 Bloomfield announced a special, exclusive and mutually rewarding arrangement with the Briton Publishing Co. The Briton Publishing Co, which was founded in 1919 by Henry Hamilton Beamish, is the longest-established purveyor of anti-semitic literature in the country, being the sole publishers of *The Protocols of the Learned Elders of Zion*. During the war years Beamish was close to the top Nazis and interned in Rhodesia because of this. Recently the company has been taken over by Timothy Tindal Robertson and, under the name of the Augustine Publishing Co, issues mainly traditionalist Catholic literature, such as the work of Archbishop Lefèbvre in conserving the Tridentine Mass. The list

---

* Now re-titled *Six Million Lost And Found*. See Historical Review Press, 19a Madeira Place, Brighton, Sussex, BN2 1TN. Its 1981 Revisionist History List also contains such offers as *For Those Who Cannot Speak* – answers to 'the distortions and misconceptions spread about National Socialism and Hitler by the controlled media by Michael McLaughlin, the leader of the British Movement (see page 52): *Anne Franks Diary – a Hoax* by Ditlieb Felderer.

includes *TFG* and a sprinkling of conspiracy material.

There is also A Hampson Services, a mail order company in Ipswich offering not only books but a wide range of Allied and Nazi militaria. It is a trading outlet of the British Movement, an openly Nazi group with many of the trappings. They offer *TFG*, described as 'an exposure of the subversive forces who under the cloak of organized Christianity finance murder, torture and terrorism . . .' and *Valkyrie*, the underground magazine of the militant and aggressive Anglo-Saxonic Church, much favoured by the National Front and similar organizations.

There are many other mailing houses, probably with only a few hundred on their address lists, but all of them spreading this 'specialist' material a little further, and this is how *TFG* is sold. (See Appendix on page 184)

The question remains as to who pays the *TFG* bill? No publisher who was unsubsidized would speculate on the basis of such a market. Private publishing, where the author pays the costs, is of course a possibility, but in this case Bernard Smith certainly has not the means.

Geoffrey Stewart-Smith, Publisher of The Fraudulent Gospel

Geoffrey Stewart-Smith's early career was that of a British 'officer and gentleman'. School at Winchester, the Royal Military Academy at Sandhurst, a commission in the Black Watch, service in Germany and Nigeria. He left the army in 1960 in order, it seems, to devote himself to politics and more especially to championing a more militant anti-communism than was fashionable at that time. For some years he worked as a journalist, first for the *Sunday Express* and then for the Economist Intelligence Unit. It was during this time that he launched the *East-West Digest*, a regular collection of articles which, to quote a recent story in *State Research* August/September 1978, 'documents the alleged activities of the Russian world conspiracy, both internationally and in this country through its British front organization, Trotskyists, anarchists, and the Labour left'. Originally, in 1964, *East-West Digest* was described as the journal of the Foreign Affairs Circle whose President was at one time the Dowager Lady Birdwood and its Vice-President Lord St Oswald, a Yorkshire landowner. The Foreign Affairs Circle has its roots among the surviving members of the McCarthyites and American China lobbyists of the 1950s, and was closely related to the Council Against Communist Aggression — alias the World

Freedom Council — alias the World Anti-Communist League, WACL for short.

In 1974, Stewart-Smith broke away from WACL after a financial disagreement about a cancelled London conference which allegedly left him with £34,000 of cancellation charges. Some journalists have thought it was because WACL was too right-wing for him.   Since then *East-West Digest* has been published by Stewart-Smith for his own publishing company Foreign Affairs Publishing Co and distributed in the same way. It should be added that there was always a strong pro-apartheid content in the journal, which ceased publication in October 1978 because of financial problems.

Stewart-Smith's Links with South Africa

Stewart-Smith had close contacts with the South African Foreign Affairs Association,[2] an organization founded to build a better image of South Africa abroad. He helped arrange visits of prominent politicians and public figures on all-expenses-paid trips to South Africa until the Foreign Affairs Association was exposed as a government front and closed down. At the time Stewart-Smith denied that he knew anything about it. He is the Director of FARI — the Foreign Affairs Research Institute — in London (within reach of MPs' lobbies) whose objectives are to carry out research into various matters of foreign affairs and defence 'right across the board' and to be in touch with similar bodies in other countries. FARI is officially financed by industry and has a budget of £70,000 a year. Its deputy director Ian Grieg has been a frequent visitor to South Africa.*

In 1974 the South African Government was widely held to be involved in attempts to discredit prominent British Liberals in the

---

* A special conference was held in Brighton in June 1978 jointly sponsored by the Institute for the Study of Conflict, FARI, Aims for Freedom and Enterprise and the American National Strategy Information Centre. C. F. de Villiers, director of the Foreign Affairs Association, soon to be exposed as a secret DOI front, was present, as was Admiral James Johnson, former head of the South African navy, plastic surgeon Dr Jack Penn and Gideon Roos of the South African Institute of International Affairs. Another guest, this time from America who was later linked with the secret project fund bid to purchase United States newspapers was Richard Mellon Scaife. (See Chapter 6.)
In the *Sunday Telegraph* 25 March 1979, Stewart-Smith said that FARI 'was in contact with many similar institutes in other countries' and added: 'Many of the institutes we deal with are government financed, and you can draw what conclusions you like from that. We do not object to it'.

election: a pamphlet was circulated linking the Liberal Party, and in particular Peter Hain, with a terrorist bomb outrage in South Africa. This pamphlet, entitled *The Hidden Face of the Liberal Party*, was published by Stewart-Smith's Foreign Affairs Publishing Company.*

The Programme to Combat Racism

At the Uppsala Assembly of the World Council of Churches in 1968, after resolutions condemning racism had been passed, there was a further determination that actions were needed in the form of practical help for the oppressed. So in 1969, at Canterbury, the Programme to Combat Racism was launched. Financial backing for the programme was to come from a special appeal to churches and individuals. The general funds of the WCC were not to be used. It is an action programme and the WCC decided that grants should be given, not only to organizations caring for the oppressed but to the oppressed themselves. From the start, grants were made to liberation movements which were involved in the armed struggle in southern Africa. These grants were for humanitarian purposes only, 'to dramatise the principle of re-distribution of income and political power and to encourage the development of cultural identity'. The grants were also made 'without control of the manner in which they are spent, and are intended as an expression of commitment.' The amounts were small in relation to the needs of such organizations, which in some cases were shouldering the burden of a sizeable population in exile. There was never any question of aid being given for military purposes. Indeed, such grants have been used for schools, medical equipment, agricultural

---

* Copies were widely distributed in a number of constituencies, including that of Bodmin Liberal Paul Tyler. Tyler said there as a lot of speculation at the time as to how the addresses were obtainied. (Paul Tyler in correspondence with author.) The content was mainly concerned with identifying the Liberals with various forms of political violence and terrorism and proving that the driving forces behind the party were politically ultra-left-wing and not the moderate ones the Liberal manifesto was promoting.

tools and the welfare needs of a large refugee community. No evidence has ever been produced that grants have been used in any other ways. Previously these movements had drawn much of their support from communist countries and were deeply affected by Sino-Soviet tensions. It is ironic that ecumenical support of liberation movements should be labelled pro-communist when, in fact, it has tended to reduce these movements' dependence on communist services and to encourage autonomy and an openness to different ideologies and relationships.

Another charge made by Bernard Smith is that the WCC is muted in its condemnation of the lack of religious freedom and human rights in communist countries. He accuses it of a double standard in focusing critical attention on southern Africa or on some of the Latin American régimes rather than on communist countries. As far as the matter of human rights in Eastern Europe is concerned, many commentators have warned how dangerous any sweeping generalizations can be about churches under communist governments. Albania is the only country where religion is forbidden. The strength of the Catholic Church in Poland was clearly demonstrated during the Pope's visit in 1979 and Church leaders from all parts of the socialist bloc take part in the work of the World Council. This diversity in government policy and in the stance of the churches is very much part of the reality of the present time. Peter Matheson wrote in the *Scotsman* on 25 October 1977: 'It ill befits us in the West to pronounce judgementally on the churches in the Socialist bloc. One returns from them always feeling rather small. They know more about the cost of discipleship in practice than we do in theory. They are not in the least in need of homilies from us about maintaining tension between Church and society. On the contrary, it is us who have to learn from them.'

Furthermore, most of the countries condemned by the WCC would call themselves 'Christian' countries. The South African government justifies apartheid with 'Christian' arguments. So the Council must take a special stand on these issues pushing Christians into an involvement with some of the most profound moral dilemmas of our time. The controversy over the PCR has generated a great deal of thoughtful reflection and writing in recent years. Readers are referred to the special pack of leaflets and notes on the PCR prepared by the British Council of Churches which contains full answers to most of the questions that occur on the subject. Similar material is available in other countries through churches which are members of the WCC.

In trying to force facts into dubious arguments, the author of *TFG* presents a hopelessly disordered image of the work of the Council. There is not even a passing reference to the fact that the WCC distributes millions of pounds every year through Inter-Church Aid for religious, humanitarian and educational work; no mention of the gamut of other departmental work which is the essence of this fellowship of churches — its church and society department wrestling with problems of science and technology — the Christian Medical Commission with its programmes of community health among peoples so far deprived of basic health services — its department of youth, and others concerned with the role of women in the church and with renewal and congregational life at grassroots level.

To Bernard Smith, the word 'Marxist' is an all-purpose smear. It should be borne in mind that many of Marx's insights have been widely accepted even by his opponents and critics: the importance of understanding how a society produces its wealth (the means of production), of asking who holds power over whom, who makes decisions, the dynamics of capitalism and so on. Smith's language only works on people who are vaguely afraid of any sort of change, and have no vocabulary for dealing with this sort of smearing political argument. To say that something is 'Marxist' is a convenient way of projecting fear and dislike, without further discussion. And Smith's ideas of what the word might mean, to judge by what he says and writes, are very crude and narrow.

Throughout the text he uses emotive words such as 'terrorists' to mean usually desperate people seeking their basic freedoms; 'fifth column' about any churchman holding a dialogue with liberation movements (the Church of Christ has often, the Lord be praised, been a 'fifth column'. That is why in South Africa courageous Christians are called communists and in the USSR they are called fascists); 'black racism' — the antithesis of the far more culpable white racism.

Donald Martin and the British League of Rights

Bernard Smith and Donald Martin have close links and the latter's association with the CAC goes all the way back to its inaugural meeting in 1974. At that time, in his newsletter

On Target, Martin wrote, 'We at the inaugural meeting of the Christian Affirmation Campaign, recognizing the humanistic and Marxist infiltration of all denominations of Christianity . . .' In the same mailing, which reached many clergymen in the London area, there was a four-page printed paper entitled *Racialism, Does Your Parson Understand His Bible?* The first two pages used mainly biblical quotes to 'justify' racial 'purity' and then warned about 'the modern red and pink clergy . . . carefully trained in their universities, colleges and seminaries by Jewish Marxist revolutionaries . . .' There was also a two-page printed paper entitled *The Destruction of the British People* which contained phrases like, 'the world is under the control of an international race who are controlled by international finance capitalism', 'this international race is atheist or agnostic believing solely in their own superiority', 'they may be defeated by accepting the true Christian Faith.'

Both these papers were distributed by Christian Attack, which is run by another of Martin's professional colleagues, Mary Stanton. There was also an order form for the Briton Publishing Company with whom Martin had a sympathetic rapport.

Scanning the material written by Donald Martin it seems that his favourite themes are racialism, anti-semitism and a dressing of extreme right-wing political views in the language of Christianity.

Searchlight — Britain's anti-fascist journal — has done careful research into Martin's past activities and present links. Those who want fuller details should consult *Searchlight*, issues 43, 48 and 49, which contain articles investigating several of the groups with which Martin is connected.

Donald Martin returned to Britain in 1970 after 14 years in Australia, during which time he had become an activist in the Australian League of Rights, run by Eric Butler. The Australian League's history stretched back to the 1930s when it grew out of the Social Credit movement of Major C H Douglas.

Social Credit, founded by Major C H Douglas, was committed to replacing the existing system of finance through banks, to one of finance through interest-free public loans. The rationale beyond this proposal was the belief that "sinister forces" (ie Jews) were able to use the power of finance to enslave societies by encouraging and facilitating catastrophic levels of public indebtedness. In Australia, Social Credit began in 1934 publishing a journal called *The New Times*, in which the anti-semitic logic of social credit theory soon became apparent; the 7th issue commenced a six part commentary on *The Protocols of the Learned Elders of Zion*, the forged tract which claims to record the discussions and decisions of the leadership of the Jewish conspiracy to take over the world. Not long after, another series of articles argued bitterly against the idea that Jews were being in any way badly treated in the Third Reich.'

(*Searchlight*, No 49)

Eric Butler first came to public notice in 1937 as a speaker and writer on behalf of the League, whose leadership he soon took over. Later, his unceasing propaganda on behalf of the fascist countries brought his activities under investigation by a government enquiry which condemned him for interfering with the war effort. Now an elderly man, his various organizations such as The Heritage Press, the Heritage Bookshop in Melbourne and the Australian Heritage Society continue to carry his books and articles and reflect his views. He travels extensively in the 'white' Commonwealth and has recently been active in the centenary celebrations of C H Douglas and the revaluation of much of his work. He is a frequent visitor to South Africa.

In the 1960s Butler began to extend the activities of the Australian League of Rights' activities overseas. In 1962 he came to London where he met A K Chesterton, then leader of the League of Empire Loyalists and later first chairman of the National Front. Subsequently Butler and Chesterton shared public platforms in Australia.

Donald Martin began organizing a British League of Rights shortly after his return to this country. He stated that he felt he owed a duty to his country, since he rejected that often-used phrase 'Britain is finished', and also because he felt that in both the long-term and short-term interests of Britain he should strenuously oppose the policy of Britain's entry into the European Economic Community. Even now he continues to work for British withdrawal from the Community.

Donald Martin's fortnightly newsletter *On Target* is a modest duplicated 12 pages. For anyone who wants it there is a printed list of principles and objectives. The 14 policy points are concerned with preserving heritage, the constitution, individual rights and liberties, support for individual enterprise. Inconspicuously at the end are the mainsprings: 'To oppose large-scale immigration of alien peoples, and to work for the maintenance of a homogeneous community.' Winding up the statement, Martin writes: 'A subscription to *On Target* helps to support these policies.' They also support his full-time activities lecturing on these affairs. *On Target*, whilst supporting the general cause of a free Britain, the anti-Common Market and anti-communist causes, does in particular support the work of the British League of Rights, the British Housewives League, and the British League for European Freedom. All[4] of them sound like representative bodies but are, in fact, vehicles for Martin's ideas.

Lady Birdwood and the World Anti-Communist League

In 1973 Donald Martin became joint leader with the Dowager Lady Jane Birdwood of the British chapter of the World Anti-Communist League (WACL), one of the most shadowy reactionary organizations.[5]

WACL receives money from the Nationalist Chinese in Taiwan and from the South Korean hierarchy and maintains a small permanent office in Seoul. In recent years ultra-right movements in Europe, the Middle East and in Latin America have entered the League. In particular, Saudi-Arabian money[6] has contributed heavily to WACL activities. WACL ideas and news of its international meetings are written up regularly in *On Target*.

The communiqué of the WACL conference at Seoul in May 1976 urged all good men and true to 'lend support to the governments of Paraguay, Guatemala, Nicaragua, El Salvador, Brazil, Uruguay and Chile for their firm struggle against Marxist-Leninist imperialism.' And in the May 1979 issue of *On Target* Donald Martin, fresh back from speaking at the WACL conference in Managua, capital of Nicaragua, and at another conference in Paraguay, praised the work of the two dictators of those countries, mingling political slogans with homilies about Christian ethics and upholding Christian civilization. Readers need no footnote to remind them that these countries have a record as amongst the most barbarous dictatorships in Latin America.

In fact, a feature in the August 1978 issue of *Searchlight* contained a warning about the kind of groups which were forming the nucleus of WACL at their Washington meeting in May of that year. One of these was MSI, (Movimento Sociale Italiano Destra Nazionale) the principal neo-fascist party of Italy whose leader Giorgio Almirante, now 62, an ex-Blackshirt and leader in Mussolini's government, was a delegate at the conference. There was also the Federation of Mexican Anti-Communists (FEMACE) which is dominated by an anti-semitic secret society called TECOS.

Several well-known racial separatists from Australia, South Africa and the United States attended and spoke at this meeting. Ivor Benson, the white South African author, was there. He is a frequent contributor to the Christian League of Southern Africa's *Encounter*, and contributing editor of the overtly racist *American Mercury*. Eric Butler, who founded the Australian League of Rights and whose influence on Donald Martin has already been referred to, was also there.

As part of this international circus both Donald Martin and Lady Birdwood were provided with useful copy for their various newsletters. They also acquired some prestige as speakers.

Background to Lady Birdwood

In her own right, the Dowager Lady Jane Birdwood has a long history of involvement in strange causes. Apart from her connection with WACL she also conducts several campaigns of her own from her home in Kensington, London. From this address she published the broadsheet *Choice* whose 1978 spring edition contained a number of sensational features about immigration and repatriation and was said to have had a circulation of 50,000 copies. *Choice* was 'opening up a second front within which it is intended to challenge, obstruct and defeat every Government, Party and Establishment policy and move that does not accord with the nation's will and falls short of our demands (on race) . . . This could well be our last chance before civil and racial strife erupt . . . above all . . . we are talking about VOTES NOT VIOLENCE, and that OUR VOTES MUST NEVER AGAIN PUT MULTIRACIAL TRAITORS INTO OFFICE.'

Another feature in *Choice* attacked the church for supporting the plural society, blaming it for the 'sickening burden of New Commonwealth immigration'. 'Churchmen', it said, 'are, alas in the forefront of all this un-Christian harassment of the indigenous population.' There are racist news stories, racist interpretations of immigration statistics, racist correspondence from readers like Henry Lord, Chairman of the Britannia Party, another extremist micro-party. There is even an advertisement for pamphlets on race published by a body called Inter-City Research Centre at the same address — another of Lady Birdwood's inventions.

Inter-City has published, for example, two booklets by Roy Bramwell, *Blatant Bias Corporation*, an attack on the BBC for its betrayal of 'kith and kin' and *The Death Tree* about the poison of immigration. Both are available through Bloomfield Books and A H Services in Ipswich.

Racism is one of the dominant strands in Lady Birdwood's thinking. In an interview with the *Darlington Evening Dispatch*, 13 October 1978, she said, 'I advocate a campaign of civil disobedience to make life more difficult for any coloured person who has arrived here in the last thirty years. I practise it already. If anyone sends a black engineer to my house I will ring back and ask for a white engineer. I think my own people have the right to do the jobs in this country . . .'

Another Birdwood brainchild is the Self Help and Current Affairs Association, which produces the occasional *British Gazette*, a title chosen deliberately from the name of the 'free' paper circulated during the General Strike of 1926 and whose purpose is to 'campaign against union tyranny', and to keep in touch with members of her grassroots Citizens Mutual Protection Union, whose vigilante-type objectives are openly flaunted. Union bashing is an area in which Lady Birdwood has been most active.

She has also been seen regularly marching with and sharing the platform at National Front events, and is quoted extensively in National Front publications. In April 1976 she headed the committee which organised the St George's Day rally in Trafalgar Square, consisting of members of the League of St George, the British Movement, the National Party, the National Front, Centre Party, the British National Party and Column 88.

Lady Birdwood has worked with Geoffrey Stewart-Smith and was a frequent contributor to his *East-West Digest*. Stewart-Smith was at one time the British Secretary of the British branch of the World Anti-Communist League through his Foreign Affairs Circle. When he resigned in 1973 complaining about increasing anti-semitism and neo-nazism, it was Lady Birdwood and Donald Martin who jointly became the leaders.

Mary Stanton and the National Assembly

A close friend and fellow campaigner of Lady Birdwood is Mary

Stanton. She was the founder of the National Assembly, a political organization whose platform included an alternative to Parliament in an Assembly consisting of handpicked nationalists from the constituencies instead of elected MPs; a rigorous anti-Common Market line; and a repatriation scheme to send blacks home. Both Lady Birdwood and George Knuppfer, another WACL activist, were closely associated with the National Assembly. There was also Joy Page, who with Monday Clubber and Tory MP Sir Ronald Bell campaigned in various anti-immigration campaigns such as the 'Halt Immigration Now' effort. For a time, the chairman of the Assembly was Geoffrey Hunt, a businessman who had been an energetic member of the extreme racialist group which sought control over the Monday Club in the early 1970s, and who stood as an independent Tory in the General Election of February 1974, in which he polled 850 votes. Bernard Smith too, is one of the Assembly's listed speakers.

Ms Stanton has, it appears, lent her flat at 25 Morpeth Mansions, Morpeth Terrace, London SW1 to a variety of rightwing causes. The National Front used the flat as their press office in the 1979 elections and although Ms Stanton claims that she is not herself a member, some of her close friends and colleagues are. Kenneth McKilliam, whose association with the National Front has been mentioned, is the author of a number of racist pamphlets which are published by Christian Attack, another Stanton front, or by the Free Society, of which she is a founding member. The Free Society, as one of its executives explains, is 'holding down a corner of the truth' and feels that its time has not yet come. Parliament, it believes, is used by political parties in mainly unlawful ways. It sees Armageddon just round the corner. It supports the British Israelite movement, and published broadsheets for Christian Attack. These are frequently distributed by Bloomfield Books, the mail order company run by Donald Martin.

The British Israel World Federation

Both Kenneth McKilliam and Mary Stanton are part of the British Israelite movement. The British Israel World Federation claims a membership of two million and maintains offices and issues publications in many parts of the world. In simple terms, the British Israel creed is that the Anglo-Saxons are the chosen people of the Bible, the ten lost tribes of Israel who got away from Assyria and came to the West. There is a long and elaborate 'proof' which relies on an interpretation of selected passages of the Bible. A huge neo-Victorian painting in the London head-quarters shows Abraham making his promise to Isaac, the Union Jack flying bravely in the background.

The Covenant people, as the British Israelites are called, have a large membership in South Africa, Australia and North America. Members may belong to any Protestant denomination, indeed they are encouraged to do so. They are all to a larger or lesser extent anti-Jew, an anti-semitism which is again provided with 'Biblical justification' because they consider the Jews as 'the remnants of Judah', a nation separate from Israel and therefore under a curse.

The religious message appeals strongly to some white nation-alists who feel threatened by immigration, by the disintegration of Empire, by Marxism, by ecumenicism and so forth. Variants of the message can be found mixed up with other elements of the fundamentalist world of Seventh Day Adventists, Millenial Dawn[7] ideas and so forth. A good example of these three fused together can be traced in the Herbert W Armstrong/Garnett Ted Armstrong/Plain Truth empire.[8] So Covenant people (though not fascists), are receptive to the messages of Afrikaner nationalists.

The British headquarters at 6 Buckingham Gate, London SW1 has a bookshop which offers a mix of British Israelite propaganda and some political books which are kept in a locked cupboard 'because of the Charity Commissioners'.

On offer was a leaflet *Beware of Ravening Wolves* attacking the WCC and praising *The Fraudulent Gospel* which they offer for sale.

A friend and regular speaker for the BIWF is National Front stalwart Kenneth McKilliam. His pamphlets *The Annihilation of Man, Revealing Anti-Christ* and *Our Nation Destroyed* are on sale on demand from the locked cupboard.

The National Message, a monthly glossy, supports the anti-WCC line of the Christian League of Southern Africa. The October 1979 issue, for example, contained an anti-terrorist piece on Rhodesia credited to the South African Federation of Covenant People, and a long article by Father Arthur Lewis of the Rhodesia Christian Group titled, 'Say No to the Crocodile', asking for a Christian mutiny on behalf of the CLSA and the RCG. In the classified advertisements K McKilliam is announced as speaker at the Streatham Norbury Library on 22 November and at HQ on 28 November 1979. The BIWF seems to maintain a regular circuit. Sir Walter Walker, former commander of NATO, addressed their congress in October 1979 on the communist threat to Western civilisation and dwelt on the value of the South African forces in maintaining the freedom of the oil routes of the world. He was fully reported in the *Daily Telegraph*, 8 October 1979.

Many people have dismissed the influence of the BIWF on public opinion as negligible. It may be so, but the quality literature spells strong financial muscle. The wide mailing lists to which the organization has access, their willingness to use material from well known right-wing extremists, the widespread presence of even one or two members in all kinds of church congregations like sickle cells in the body, all put a question mark over their activities and invite vigilance.

Similarly, the presence of a National Front activist like Kenneth McKilliam in several of the organizations which have been described forces one to look more closely at their aims. But McKilliam is not only a National Front stalwart of long standing but the chairman of the Ashford, Kent, National Front group and a lay reader of the Church of England for over 30 years. The introduction to an article by him in the *League Review* of August 1978, the journal of the extreme right-wing League of St George, had this to say about him. 'Captain McKilliam is well known to patriots in Britain. He is a National Front Prospective Parliamentary Candidate and a keen supporter and speaker for the British Israel Christian Church. He is renowned for his study of Freemasonry and the International Conspiracy to destroy Britain.' His booklets are indeed racist and anti-semitic and a sounding-board for the great crusade against the world conspiracy of evil, atheistic communism, the syndicate of international bankers and the Zionist-Soviet network to dominate the world and destroy Christian civilization.

Conclusion

The different elements of the ultra-right form subtle and different patterns of prejudice to suit the group and the occasion. The names of the groups sound respectable and reassuring. Complex ideas are simplified into simple 'truths' and repetition reinforces their credibility. The organizations discussed above are some of the connections which Bernard Smith and the Christian Affirmation Campaign keep in Britain. It does not necessarily follow that the ideas and beliefs of each group are shared with each other. However, as has been illustrated, they provide each other with support for common ends which includes the possibility of hidden finance and they co-operate or take part in each other's meetings, publicize each other's written ideas, share address lists and common mailings. A common ingredient in many of these groups is open partisanship or at least a flirtation with the ideas of the extreme right movements in British politics, the National Front and its even more extreme cousins such as the League of St George and the British Movement.

References

1. These targets are the subjects of three leaflets, *Christian Aid: the Politics of Charity*, an attempt to prove that Christian Aid funds terrorists; *The Spiritual Fifth Column*, on how the churches are supposed to be betraying the West; *Revolution and the British Churches* in which the churches are linked to the revolutionary left.

2. The director of the FAA, C F de Villiers, was a participant in the Brighton Conference of July 1978, jointly sponsored by Geoffrey Stewart-Smith's FARI and the Institute for the Study of Conflict. Also present were Admiral James Johnson, former head of the South African Navy, South African plastic surgeon Dr Jack Penn and Gideon Roos of the South African Institute of International Affairs. The *Guardian*, 23 November 1978, reported that the FAA had been disbanded by order of South Africa's Foreign Minister, Pik Botha.

3. See *Searchlight*, No 48, June 1979. The British League of Rights, *On Target*, Bloomfield Books, the British Housewives League, the British League for European Freedom, all share the same address. The British League of Rights lists as Patron, Air Vice-Marshal Don Bennett; National Director, Donald Martin ; Assistant National Secretary, Mrs Caroline Hicks. *On Target* lists Editor and Publisher, Donald Martin; Assistant Editor, Mrs Caroline Hicks. British League for European Freedom lists Chairman, Donald Martin; Vice-Chairman, the Dowager Lady Birdwood; General Secretary, Mrs Caroline Hicks. Bloomfield Books lists as its Principal, Donald Martin; Assistant, Mrs Caroline Hicks.

4. This may be gleaned from an article by Peter Dale Scott in the American magazine *Ramparts* in November 1973 entitled 'From Dallas to Watergate — the longest cover-up', which examined fresh evidence about the killing of President Kennedy. The Warren Commission Report stated that Lee Harvey Oswald and his Russian wife Marina were met in New York not by the FBI or the CIA but by 'Spas T Raikin, a representative of the Traveler's Aid Society' (R 713). But as Scott points out, the FBI interviews to the Commission did not reveal that Spas Raikin was also the Secretary-General of the American Friends of the anti-Bolshevik

He was adviser to a body called the British Military Volunteer Force which at various times, attempted to bring together a mercenary force to go into Vietnam to assist the United States and into Zaire, Biafra, the Yemen and Rhodesia. Publicity given by Southern TV in 1967 to the African ventures lost one of the British ex-officers involved, Major J A Friend, his Conservative candidacy. According to Peoples News Service, 17 April 1979, Lady Jane Birdwood was also involved in the BMVF.

Bloc of Nations, a small, active group of right-wing refugee East Europeans who were in close touch with the FBI and Army Intelligence — and at the same time with the Gehlen spy set-up in West Germany, the nationalist régime in Taiwan, right-wing Cubans such as Carlos Bringuier, a contact of Oswald's, and other elements of a shadowy 'World Anti-Communist League'. Scott goes on to say that this WACL had contacts with US anti-communists in New Orleans, in the same building used by Oswald at Camp Street, which was also used by the CIA's Cuban Revolutionary Council. He also refers back to his previous book *The War Conspiracy* (Bobbs, Merrill 1972) in which he had pointed out that Raikin's personal correspondents in Taiwan (the Asian Peoples' Anti-Communist League (APACL) were intelligence agents involved in the Taiwan government's narcotics traffic. The accusation was given weight whrn the Laotian delegate to APACL was arrested in Paris in 1971 carrying 60 kilograms of high-grade heroin worth 13.5 million US dollars on the streets of New York.

5. See *Searchlight*, 4 and 9 July 1979 and *Washington Post*, 28 May 1978 both headed 'Neo Fascists Out in Force about WACL International Conference'. The Saudis contributed about $ 75,000 towards the costs of the conference.

6. Millenial Dawn was the movement out of which the Jehovah's Witnesses arose.

7. Herbert W Armstrong used to have a regular programme on Radio Luxemburg in the 1950s called World Today which had as a spin-off a glossy give-away magazine *The Plain Truth*. His son Garnett Ted Armstrong led a movement called the 'Worldwide Church of God' which was a fusion of all these ideas with the British Israel Movement.

3. The Knuckle and Boot Boys

The National Front

The National Front's aim during the 1979 British parliamentary elections, as on previous occasions, was to present itself as a respectable alternative party, somewhat to the right of the Conservatives maybe, but a patriotic party which sincerely championed the *white* indigenous people of Britain, whose vital interests had, the NF maintained, been unjustly neglected by the other parties.

In its 1979 election leaflet and in other publications it called for the repatriation of Britain's coloured immigrant population, using force if need be. It wanted Britain to leave the Common Market. It called for support for apartheid in South Africa, and for a wide-ranging programme of tough measures to ensure decency and 'law and order' in this country.

Below the veneer of respectability the NF assumes around election time, its main platform remains racism and violence. Here are a few quotes by NF leaders:

> 'The day that our followers lose their ability to hate will be the day that they lose their power and their will to achieve anything worthwhile at all.' (John Tyndall, *Spearhead*, September 1975)

> 'The knuckle and the boot must be used to defend the streets.' (Martin Webster, *Harpers and Queen*, February 1977)

> 'The greatest danger this country has ever faced is that it has imported millions of aliens who are members of backward primitive races and whose large-scale racial intermixture with the indigenous Anglo-Saxon would not only put an end to the British as a distinct and unique ethnic entity, but would produce an inferior mongrel breed and a regressive and degenerate culture of tropical squalor.' (Richard Verrall, *Spearhead*, October 1976)

> 'The National Front has done much good work in ruining good race relations in the community, and I am proud of my contribution to this work.' (Malcolm Smith, member of NF National Directorate, *Kilburn Times*, 25 November 1977)

> 'The Jew is like a maggot feeding on a body in an advanced state of decay.' (John Tyndall, *New Statesman*, 4 November 1977)

47

The literature illustrating the resemblance between the ideas and tactics of the German National Socialists and the new National Front and its offshoots is abundant. The NF and its followers are not ashamed to make statements on public platforms, in interviews and in leaflets, broadsheets and newsletters.

The Historical Background

After the death of Hitler in 1945 and the overthrow of the Nazi movement in Europe, the evidence of genocide in the concentration camps and the documentation of the Nuremburg Trials, Nazism was considered to be extinguished. The world would never forget, it was said, and there was a strong feeling that no such evil could ever return. Yet within a few years the seeds were sprouting once again. In Britain, Oswald Mosley returned to his soap box under the banner of the Union Movement. His influence was negligible but there followed a succession of neo-fascist organizations: the League of Empire Loyalists founded in 1954 by A K Chesterton, a founder member of Mosley's pre-war British Union of Fascists, and an obsessive anti-semite; the White Defence League formed by Colin Jordan; the British National Party, which came from a merger between John Tyndall and John Bean's National Labour Party and Colin Jordan's body in 1960; Colin Jordan's further breakaway, the National Socialist Movement, formed in 1962 by John Tyndall and Martin Webster with its rallying cry of 'Free Britain from Jewish Control'.

In October 1962, the public learned of the discovery of the paramilitary 'Spearhead' group, and its cache of arms. This led to prison sentences for Tyndall, Jordan and others.[1] In 1963 Tyndall was released and started his own Greater British Movement, in which he was joined by Martin Webster. In 1964 Tyndall began *Spearhead* magazine which he still owns and runs through Albion Press.

The National Front began operating in 1966 when the GBM was joined by Chesterton's League of Empire Loyalists and soon after by the Patriotic Party, the True Tories, branches of the Anglo-Rhodesian Society and a section of the Racial Preservation Society. In 1968 the NF started to 'kick its way into the headlines'. After Martin Webster became activities organizer in 1969, the tactics of the Front became so violent that even A K Chesterton was disturbed and resigned in 1971. He was replaced for a short time by John O'Brien, a former Conservative who had resigned from the party to start a 'Powell for Premier' group in 1968. He in turn was ousted by John Tyndall within 18 months. In his resignation letter O'Brien wrote: 'There is a small caucus working within the National Front attracted by the trappings and ideologies of foreign nationalisms from the past. These persons see Britain's future best served by her becoming a rigidly administered, authoritarian police state. They sought to use me as a docile puppet behind whose respectability they could operate from the shadows.'

1972 was the year when General Amin's action against the Asian community in Uganda provided the NF with its best recruiting platform to date and they exploited it for all it was worth. Martin Walker in his book *The National Front* wrote:

'The Heath Government's 1971 Immigration Act had outflanked a considerable proportion of the anti-immigrant feeling in the Conservative Party in the country. By taking the honourable decision to grant the refugees (Ugandan Asians) free entry and assistance in resettlement, the Government made itself vulnerable to anti-immigration sentiment. So the third issue the NF was able to exploit was the "feebleness" of the Heath government — an argument which was to prove particularly effective within the Monday Club.'

There were immediate marches and protest rallies in which other groups also took part. At a rally and march to Smith Square on 7 September 1972 Joy Page of the Immigration Control Association and Air-Vice-Marshal Donald Bennett (whose other interests include being a patron of the British League of Rights) spoke. The Monday Club was courted. On 30 September 1972 Lady Birdwood was on a NF platform in Blackburn representing her own Anti-Immigration Co-Ordinating Committee. Earlier in the month there was an important Monday Club rally in Central Hall, Westminster, stiffened by some 400 NF supporters who afterwards led a march to Downing Street. A number of important Monday Clubbers joined the movement.

The NF Connection with the Monday Club

The Monday Club was begun in 1961 by a group of Young Conservatives who were dismayed by Harold MacMillan's 'Wind of Change' speech and believed that the party's drift to the left had gone too far. It was dedicated to 'traditional Conservative principles' and saw itself as a ginger group within the party, not a breakaway faction. Its gut sentiment was anti-immigrant and anti-communist. On several counts, therefore, its members would be expected to see eye to eye with NF policies.

In the late 1960s the centre of gravity in the Club moved even further to the right. Although Enoch Powell was never a member, the Club came heavily under his influence — it was the time of his passionate campaign against Commonwealth immigration. In the run-up to the 1970 election came his famous speech in which he spoke of a wide conspiracy of forces within Britain aiming at its actual destruction and accused an invisible but all-powerful minority of trying to hoodwink the majority. His reference to the process of immigration as an 'invasion' and to areas of immigrant settlement as 'foreign areas', combined with mystical concepts of nationhood and national character, earned him the label of racist, and the admiration of many NF followers.

Powellism seen as an injection of new political principles into a dull Conservative credo did not develop, but Powell's political clout made gossip and rumour against immigration a subject for serious political discussion. He thus inadvertently helped boost NF fortunes and reinforced their prejudices.

Nevertheless, at this period the Monday Club with its strong pro-Powell faction was an important link for the NF. It 'serves a useful purpose as a rallying point and recruiting ground' (*Spearhead*). Undoubtedly there are still members of the NF who are also members of the Monday Club, and its position is still passionately anti-immigration and pro-white minority rule in southern Africa, but since the late 1970s the executive of the Club has attempted to stop any official association. For a short time towards the end of the 1960s and early 1970s there was a danger that NF members and their allies might take over the Club. They used their influence to get into its well printed and circulated publications list. Monday Clubber Bernard Smith was sharpening his claws on the 'leftist bias' of the church leadership in a pamphlet called *The Crooked Conscience* long before he founded the Christian Affirmation Campaign. George K Young wrote the Monday Club's most celebrated pamphlet, *Who Goes Home? Immigration and Repatriation* (1969), in which he warmly supported the Powell line.

In 1973 G K Young attempted to gain the chairmanship, with the help of the Powellite and National Front supporters in the Club. Young's career up to that time had been an unusual one. He was a former journalist who had served in Military Intelligence during the Second World War before joining the Foreign Office. From there he moved to the Ministry of Defence and rose to be deputy head of MI6. In 1961 he left the service to become a merchant banker and he is at present European Director for Kleinwort Benson in the City.

For a time he was involved with General Walter Walker's scheme for a private army to help run the country in the case of large-scale industrial dispute and he was also at one time a prospective Conservative candidate in Brent East. At the Monday Club he was involved in various leadership intrigues but his main concern seems always to have been the promotion of anti-immigration groups and policies. In this activity he worked closely with Beryl (Bee) Cardew, a member of the Monday Club executive who was meetings secretary and who also ran the Powellite Association. Ms Cardew later dropped the Powellite Association and joined the National Front. Young was also on friendly political terms with Kay Tomlin, a Monday Clubber and member of the Anglo-Rhodesian Society who was mixed up with John Tyndall and the NF in the late 1960s in an attempt to oust the then Tory MP Tom Iremonger from his seat in Ilford North.

G K Young was also involved in setting up funds and providing the organization to make the racist anti-immigration film *England Our England* for the British Campaign to Stop Immigration, one of a host of organizations which Martin Walker[2] lists as receiving NF 'manpower and support'. Proposals to turn Counterblast, the company created to make the film, into a wider-ranging communications group did not materialize, but the showing of part of the film in BBC's Open Door programme during 1976 certainly helped keep the controversy in the headlines and re-opened the debate about the way the media handled extremist organizations whose avowed policy was 'to kick themselves into the headlines'. There was also a project to create an umbrella organization with representatives of the Monday Club, the National Front and the Stop Immigration Campaign.

In 1973 the NF's hopes of seizing control of the Monday Club were dashed; the moderates gathered their strength, the hardline racists were defeated and G K Young's bid for the chairmanship failed. Nevertheless, Young has not stopped campaigning on the same sort of issues. He emerged in 1979 as a member of the far right Conservative group called Tory Action. This group publishes a bulletin called *Round Robin*, whose

51

columns are the host to sentiments found only in the NF's *Spearhead* magazine. The February 1979 issue carries a reprint of an article on 'patriotism' by G K Young which originally appeared in the *Liverpool Newsletter* — the private publication of Anthony Cooney, who supports the National Front and its more extremist rival the British Movement together with Social Credit. An extract from Young's article is illuminating:

> 'While the British are denied a sense of solidarity and threatened by law if they object, the alien wedge — as Lord Denning described it — which has been driven deep into the heart of the nation, is allowed and even encouraged to maintain its racial and cultural identities. The Jewish community practises APARTHEID and in the Jewish newspapers the diatribes against any patriotic manifestation take on a rising hysterical note. We look for a focus of loyalty but on every occasion the Monarch has to be photographed beaming at a piccaninny while Prince Philip and Prince Charles caper about in yarmulkas.'

As *Searchlight* magazine was quick to point out, Tory Action, with its raw edge of racism and anti-semitism, seems to be an attempt to resurrect the old alignment of extremists in the party and beyond it, which tried to build itself around a Monday Club purged of 'softliners' some seven years ago.

This digression shows how tangled are the skeins of right-wing political groupings in Britain in recent years.

The British Movement

Just as the NF came together from many factions and small parties, so other factions started breaking away from it almost immediately. For some members the NF was not tough enough: they needed another kind of outlet. One such group was the British Movement, started by Colin Jordan in 1968 and now run by a Merseysider Michael McLaughlin with a membership of about 3,000.

The BM affects to see the NF as 'kosher fascists' because in its attempts to remain respectable it has denied being anti-semitic. The BM makes no bones about its Hitlerian legacy. In its paper the *British Patriot* it hammers the conspiracy theories of Zionism and international Jewry and urges the view that the history of Nazi Germany has been widely misrepresented, that the facts of the holocaust are lies and that six million Jews never died. *Did Six Million Really Die? — The Truth at Last*, by Richard Harwood, attempts to prove that the 'allegation' is utterly unfounded, 'an invention of post-war propaganda'. The book is distributed by Robin Beauclair through his mailing catalogue *Historical Review Press* and boasts a million copies sold in 40 countries since it was published in 1974.

The BM organizes street events in which members can be seen in a blue shirt and black trouser uniform. Selected members are recruited into a 'leader guard' and given special training. There are links with mercenary training agencies[3] who have been looking for recruits to fight in Southern Africa. The BM has widespread links with fascist and neo-Nazi movements in the United States and in Western Europe. It is a member of the co-ordinating body called the New European Order and is affiliated to the World Union of National Socialists (WUNS) and to the White People's Alliance. With the League of St George the BM organized a contingent to the annual fascist rally at Diksmuide in Belgium.

One of the principal sources of income for the British Movement is the sale of literature, tapes, records and pre-war Nazi and other military regalia by mail order catalogue and through a number of shops. These include Mary Calland, who runs the women's section of the BM and who is a partner in a record shop at Shotton on Deeside; Military World of Ipswich which has an international mail order catalogue including Nazi militaria; A Hampson Services which offers an international catalogue in association with Military World and advertises mailing lists, delivery services, IBM typing and duplicating. Their mailing catalogue contains Bernard Smith's *The Fraudulent Gospel*.

Salvo, published from the same address by Victor Norris and his wife using the pen-name of R J Frimley, started serialising *TFG* in the autumn of 1979. The first two issues contained, in addition to the Smith material, a viciously racist cartoon and another lampooning the World Council of Churches for supposed gun-running to SWAPO — the Namibian liberation movement — commendation for *News of the New World*, a white supremacist South African journal, a statistical set of 'facts' from official South African sources which were used by the Christian League of Southern Africa in a leaflet circulated in Britain last year and a piece describing the 'Bilderberger Conference conspiracy', plus other overtly racist pieces.

Valkyrie was another broadsheet emanating from the same address in Ipswich edited by Tony Bentley, which was believed to be another pseudonym of Victor Norris. Its flavour was similar to that of *Salvo*, and they have now been combined.

In April 1980, in an exchange of letters in the church press and elsewhere, Bernard Smith declared that he was in no way ashamed that his booklet should appear from this kind of source. 'It is all good publicity', he said. Victor Norris denied that he had any connection with the British Movement or that he was in any way racist or linked with any neo-fascist organization. The file on Norris contradicts this statement.

The Connection with Victor Norris

On 1 October 1968, in an article in the *Colchester Evening Gazette*, Norris, speaking to Colchester Young Liberals, said that he was the leader of 'a Right-Wing Group of members very intense in their objection to immigration and what they considered the inevitable doom of Britain as a multi-racial society if immigration continued'. This group called itself the 5000 Group. He told his audience that 'it was planned with an army of a thousand to invade and take over the University and then demolish it.' 'The University was chosen', he said, 'as being a vanguard of communism'.

In his speech, the article went on, Norris said the only way to achieve power was through bloody revolution. He saw present left-inspired demonstrations leading to anarchy, on which the 5000 Group would swoop to take power to restore law and order to the clamouring working class. He also said that his group was not a political party, although naturally they would support a right-wing form of government.

A small number of committed fascists seem to move from one group to another in a never ending quest for situations they can exploit. The mid-winter 1978 issue of another magazine, *Raven Banner*, gave further evidence of regrouping. Many of the contributors are well-known on the Nazi scene — B Baldwin, former British Movement member and organizer of Column 88 para-military activities, John Yeowell, League of St George member.

The Racial Preservation Society

The Racial Preservation Society pre-dates these organizations, having been set up about 1964 by a group of right-wingers living in Brighton. The founders included Jimmy Doyle, a local Conservative Party member and the Hancock family, consisting of A V Hancock, a long-standing supporter of Oswald Mosley, his German wife, and their son.[4] They were joined by Raymond Bamford, a wealthy scion of the famous engineering company of that name, and by Robin Beauclair who had earned a fortune in property and catering. A mass circulation broadsheet, professionally printed, called *RPS News* or *The British Independent* was published and circulated. Its offensive content of a deeply racist hue led to a mass of complaints and a court case. The Lewes[5] Trial, as it became known, brought under the new race relations legislation, failed and exposed the weakness of the Act in dealing with cleverly written racist propaganda. Probably as a result, the RPS has seen as its major objective an ongoing campaign against what it calls the 'Race Industry'. Its aim, it declares, is to expose racist anti-white individuals and bodies and to press for the abolition of such bodies.[6] In the period following the foundation of the National Front in 1967, many members of the RPS were drawn away but the RPS re-emerged in 1974 in connection with meetings and actions of the Northern League with which the Hancocks were involved. The Northern League first met in Britain, but its overtly Nazi colouring led to violence and its HQ was moved to Holland and then to West Germany where it attracted former Nazis and their collaborators.

Today, the RPS publishes a racially provocative broadsheet called *Race and Nation*. It has a catalogue of booklets and reprints and is believed to be behind the Wessex Group which advertises racist booklets through a coded London box number.[7]

In 1977, a National Front claim that some Church of England ministers were members caused a small press sensation as reporters rushed hither and thither trying to name names and stir up controversy in the church.

In the *Sunday Times*, 16 October 1977, the NF claimed that six Church of England clergymen, a number of Free Church ministers and one Roman Catholic monk had joined them, but no one was named. The media spotlight fell briefly on one of these clergymen, the Rev Terry Spong. He had recently been appointed prison chaplain at Brixton prison, an area with a large black population, after serving as prison chaplain at Gwelo gaol in Rhodesia. The Bishop of Southwark protested to the prison authorities and Spong resigned before there was a risk of a head-on clash. The *Guardian*, 17 October 1977, reported him as saying, 'My Christian ideals are that I am proud to be white and British. I am appalled by what has happened to the country of my birth.'

Anti-fascist groups have been aware for some time of a small number of clergy attracted by authoritarianism. One such was the Rev Peter Eugene Blagden-Gamlen, Vicar of Eastchurch on the Isle of Sheppey. In a letter to the *Church Times* on 11 September 1964, he urged the launching of a 'definitely Christian Keep Britain White Campaign' and maintained that miscegenation is a grave sin and that this is clearly taught in the Bible. When he celebrated the jubilee of his ordination several years ago, the National Front were represented at the mass.[8]

Another open National Front supporter has been the Rev Brian Green of the Zoar Free Grace Baptist Church in Hounslow, who stood in the 1970 General Election as NF candidate in Islington; he took part in an anti-Catholic demonstration in 1971 outside Buckingham Palace, for which he was fined £25, and supported Enoch Powell's 'pay them to go home' policy. Since 1972 he has often led the unofficial service for the Rhodesian white dead, held by the National Front on Remembrance Day. He has published a summary of the notorious *The Protocols of the Learned Elders of Zion* — the fraudulent anti-semitic history of world conspiracy. He is the General Secretary of the British Council of Protestant Churches, a small, fanatical anti-ecumenical group of which the Rev Ian Paisley is Vice-President, not to be confused with the British Council of Churches which represents all the main-line Protestant churches.

There is also the Rev George Nicholson, the Vicar of Burghfield and now 83 years old. Active in racist groups since the early 1950s, Nicholson is the author of various pamphlets advocating racism. He supports South Africa's 'racial mission' and sees his God as 'the great racial discriminator.' He too has officiated at the National Front unofficial Remembrance Day service at the Cenotaph in Whitehall.[9]

The Churches Fight Back

It took the churches many years to recognize the central racist message of the NF as an evil which had to be challenged and overcome. Even when various Christian writers pointed out similarities between the development of the NF and its smaller rivals with the rise of the German Nazi movement in the 1930s, there was still a great reluctance on the part of the churches to go beyond a general call to greater racial harmony. Then came Lewisham.

On 13 August 1977 the Front organized a march through the streets of Lewisham, which has a large black population, a high unemployment record and considerable poverty. It was deliberate provocation. Civic and church leaders tried to persuade the police to ban the march and mobilized a peaceful protest march under the banner of the All Lewisham Campaign against Racism and Fascism when the plea failed. The result of the NF's afternoon parade was predictable: there was a violent confrontation and by the end of the afternoon 211 people had been arrested and 112 injured. In his speech to supporters in Lewisham John Tyndall said:

> 'When we win in this country and win we will, there are going to be some mighty changes . . . I'll tell you where one of the biggest is going to come. There's going to be a good sweep out of the Church (cheers and cries of "start tomorrow"). And we're going to send these political priests, the whole ragbag lot of them, off to Russia where they belong. We'll put in their place Christian leaders who will do the job they are supposed to do — which is to look after the morality and the spiritual welfare and the cohesion of the British people.'

In the space of a couple of months during the winter of 1977 there was a sudden spate of warnings from church leaders that the racial policies of the NF and other extremist offshoots were incompatible with the Christian faith. There were statements from the Archbishop of Canterbury, the Roman Catholic Council of Bishops, the British Council of Churches and the Church of Scotland, attacking racism. In an open letter in 1978, published by the Board of Deputies of British Jews in *They Stand Condemned*, the Bishops of Southwark and Woolwich warned:

> 'The National Front is an evil cancer in the body of Britain. No matter what our politics may be — right, left, or centre — we must stand shoulder to shoulder in our opposition to its wickedness. No Christian who has an informed understanding of the scriptures can support it. Its attitude towards racism and to much else is utterly condemned by the Gospel of Our Lord Jesus Christ. It is evil — as evil as Hitler and the Nazis.'

Hundreds of thousands of British Christians have signed the BCC's 'Affirmation Against Racism', witnessing their rejection of the teachings of the fascist front. But of course, the ideas and actions of the NF are not vanquished by statements alone. Professor John Hick, Professor of Theology at Birmingham University, wrote:

'At a time when the country's influence in the world is sharply reduced and when we are plagued by soaring unemployment, a high level of inflation and deep worries about the future, many confused and anxious people are ready to grasp at simple solutions and find relief in venting their anger upon a visible scapegoat. In post-Weimar Germany, the scapegoat was the Jews; in post-war Britain it is the black and brown people who have come here from the Caribbean islands and the Indian sub-continent.'[11]

In answer to NF calls for the preservation of racial purity, John Hick wrote:

'There is no rational alternative to the attempt to make a success of a pluralistic Britain which includes people of different colours and creeds and ethnic origins. We have to create a fresh phase of the ever-changing civilisation of the British Isles, including in the new mix the cultural contributions of the Caribbean and India, Pakistan and Bangladesh — themselves deeply influenced by Britain in the past and now exerting their own reciprocal influence.

'In this situation the churches have an immense opportunity for Christian leadership. Indeed this can — if they have the vision to see it — be their distinctive contribution to the national life in the last decades of the twentieth century. They still have the resources to take a decisive lead in helping our traditional white society, including both church members and other men and women of good will, to face the problems and opportunities of the new situation. This is perhaps the most obvious application of the Christian faith to the life of Britain today: and by their success or failure here the British churches will no doubt be judged in the perspective of history.'

There have been fresh initiatives since that piece was written. The Anti-Nazi League has mobilized community concern and established a new understanding of the issues. Within the churches Christians against Racism and Fascism (CARAF) has mounted vigils and multi-racial meetings, on a more intimate scale. Nevertheless too little is being done. The latent racism of the white community in Britain has been fanned into flames by racist fringe groups working on the fear of terrorism by 'black guerrillas' against white folk; wedges of hate have been driven between young people of different races by propaganda about genetic inferiority and fears about competition for jobs; antagonism between black and coloured youth and the police has been allowed to grow; suspicions that the administration of the law may, in certain circumstances, have a most unjust colour-bias have developed. All these require urgent Christian understanding and action.

Blue handbills from the National Front entitled *CHURCH LEADERS — who've forgotten their duties* were given away in the London area during the early summer of 1979. They hit the streets in the weeks leading up to and including Christian Aid's traditional nationwide appeal week on behalf of its work. The timing was no coincidence.

In stark terms the leaflet suggested that if your church was affiliated to the World Council of Churches, you were, by contributing to the collection plate, helping terrorists like those who killed missionaries and their families at Umtali, Rhodesia, in June 1978. The photo used to create a stronger reaction of fear and disgust was of a young woman and baby — the same one which had been used some time earlier by the Christian League of Southern Africa for a similar handbill with a similar message. The use of gruesome photos of real or alleged atrocities against whites in southern Africa, accompanied by misleading stories, was part of official Rhodesian policy to keep alive feelings of outrage amongst white 'kith and kin' in Britain. This type of material was also used by other racist groups as part of their effort to exacerbate racial tensions in the community and to intensify support from the white minority in southern Africa. Church contributions to the humanitarian programmes of the liberation movements in southern Africa gave these groups the excuse to accuse Church leaders of taking up politics 'instead of looking after the souls of men and women'.

The NF leaflets were sighted in Forest Hill, in the East End of London and in Regent Street in London's West End. No doubt there were other pockets of distribution. Indeed in the May 1979 issue of *Spearhead*, the monthly NF magazine, which has an estimated circulation of some 5,000, there was a feature on the street leafleting of the Umtali mission handbill around All Soul's Church in Langham Place, London W1, as a fashionable congregation was arriving for matins. The event was jokily compared to a grouse shoot, with lots of ho-hoing about potting them in the left wing.

It was not Christianity the NF was attacking, the feature emphasized, only those who abuse it and misinterpret it, ie the multi-racialists of the Church of England 'hellbent on bogus equality and a racial disaster'. It was not the first time the NF had attempted to block church efforts to collect for overseas development projects. 'We want Church leaders who will do the job they are supposed to do, which is to look after the morality of the people, and not the Third World', Martin Webster, NF organizer, said.

In May 1977 *Spearhead* published a scurrilous piece by Bernard Smith of the CAC attacking 'the subversives of Christian Aid' who gave grants to *black* Africans who might be terrorists, to Chilean refugees who were 'a motley collection of revolutionary parasites' and to the BCC's Race Relations Unit, which supported Black Power groups which were racially aggressive. While Smith does not seem to be closely involved with the NF today, many of his basic ideas echo Tyndall's. Both Tyndall and Smith denounce as 'political priests' those whose denunciation of racism and fascism stem from the Gospel. Both see Britain's clergy as race traitors. Both support apartheid. Both condemn the permissive society. A close analysis of their utterances would find many other parallels.

This is not the place to develop in detail the thinking or actions of the churches to combat the NF. Readers are urged to read an excellent short essay by John Hick, the Professor of Theology at Birmingham University, entitled *Christianity and Race in Britain Today*, published by AFFOR which presents a complex subject in simple digestible terms. In 1978, the Board of Deputies of British Jews produced a pack of material for all those who need to face and expose NF material or activities. It contains a booklet of essays and quotations, *They Stand Condemned — What every Christian should know about the National Front*, which goes swiftly and accurately to the heart of the matter, and lists many suggestions for combating the NF.

Where people understand the truth of the NF, its hateful influence can be successfully resisted. The town of Leicester in the United Kingdom is an outstanding example. During the 1976 local elections, the NF fought every Council seat, winning 18.5 per cent of the vote and coming near to winning several seats. But in recent elections Leicester was the first city to organize a united campaign to stop the NF, with church groups, trade union leaders, businessmen, politicians and civic-minded citizens burying their differences in a concerted effort to educate ordinary people about the dangers of the National Front. In this election the NF percentage dropped by a third.

The group has continued to work since 1977 and its efforts have been rewarded by seeing the percentage of the NF vote drop to 2.4 per cent in 1979. One of the main reasons for this was that race and immigration were never allowed to become central issues in the campaign.

Other recommended texts are listed in the bibliography at the back of this work.

The NF Connection with South Africa

While tracing connections between groups in Britain and South African interests, what about the National Front? In a recent press report it was revealed that in 1964, the Broederbond, the powerful Afrikaner secret society which dominates the power structures of South Africa, decided to expand its activities 'to manipulate opinion makers and establish liaison with sympathetic professional and power groups in the West'. A new book *The Broederbond*,[12] by Ivor Wilkins and Hans Strydom, based on leaked documents, shows how this new role has been developed. It shows how Broederbond activities have been extended 'into African and Western countries where liberals and Communists have joined the battle with Afrikanerdom and the white nation'. The links to be forged had to be with 'believing Protestants and convinced nationalists'. Who, one wonders, would be their natural allies in Britain? The NF has always seen itself as a Christian and a nationalist party. The march to the Cenotaph on Remembrance Day in honour of the white Rhodesian dead was 'a religious one'. Tyndall expressed his view thus:

> 'The white settlers fighting to retain their position are fighting for our cause and our future, the future of British civilisation the world over . . . White Rhodesians and South Africans should be under no illusion; they should recognize that their only true friends in this country are those who are prepared to speak out openly in defence of their right to stay in power for all time . . .'[13]

Tyndall has always advocated a version of the apartheid system for Britain.

> 'If ever the basic character of the British people were to alter and their inherent qualities be lost, then no amount of improvement in their institutions would avail against the certainty of a dark future . . . We therefore oppose racial integration and stand for racial separateness . . .'[14]

The NF not only plays the South African tune, but is prepared to treat enemies of apartheid as its own. Churches working for social justice in southern Africa are 'enemies' of white civilization. The WCC's support for liberation movements is 'traitorous' to the white race.

There is an active South African branch of the National Front, and John Tyndall has visited South Africa to address meetings and confer with colleagues. In *Spearhead* magazine Noel Hunt, described as 'our man in southern Africa', writes regularly on South African and Rhodesian affairs. There are publishing links with the Federation of the Covenant People, the South African British Israelite body in Johannesburg who have produced, among other mainly racist material, the heavily pro-white leaflet *The Myths That Destroyed Rhodesia*. One of the NF dreams is of Britain leading a new, white Commonwealth in which the British will stand side by side with the white folk of South Africa and Rhodesia to write a glorious new chapter of white Christian civilization.[15] One of the Afrikaner Nationalist dreams is to be recognized as the people who preserved the civilization of the white man.

Despite these many signs of sympathy and support which the National Front leadership has shown for the minority white régime of South Africa and the former Smith régime in Rhodesia, no evidence has yet been uncovered to show any direct connection between the NF and the secret South African G-Fund.[16]

There is however some evidence that NF local organizers receive mailings from the CLSA and use this material in their campaigning. A letter in the *Haslingden Observer* on 14 June 1980 from the North West Regional Organizer of the NF, David Ridley, attacking Christian Aid admits that his 'facts' come from the CLSA.

The NF does, however, expose the raw nerve of latent racism in British society and official South African information services glorify each item of evidence to highlight British hypocrisy on matters of racism.

A final word. In the summer General Election of 1979, the National Front fielded 303 candidates and received 190,063 votes. No candidate got anywhere near a seat in Parliament, but it remained the fourth largest political party. The percentage of votes in those constituencies which the Front contested dropped from an average of 2.9 per cent in the 1974 election to 1.3 per cent. For the Front it was a disaster, although the leadership commented that they only participated in the election 'for the platform it would allow us, for publicity and member recruiting'. (John Tyndall to an audience of American Nazis in Atlanta, Georgia in July 1979.)

Since then several commentators have warned that the NF may be down but not out. Many of the candidates were young and therefore unlikely to have personal experiences or memories of the Hitler period. There is also a strong cadre of teenagers who get their kicks from street activities and demonstrations and will continue to be attracted to the NF as long as it takes to the streets for 'show' events; a chance to use the knuckle and boot.

Webster himself admits that 'the social base of the NF is made up of the desperate and dispossessed'. They patronize a party for which racism is the only issue that really matters. As Webster puts it, the NF will wait 'for power in a situation of national economic catastrophe and a collapse of law and order'.[17]

The mixture remains very volatile. One element is the undoubted decline in recent years of consensus politics in Britain. Part of this is shown in the increase in militant forms of protest and outbursts of extremist violence from the many small sects and campaigns on the political fringe, none of whom are able to offer an effective challenge to society. Other elements are the international economic chaos and the major recession with its growing unemployment, increasing inflation and deteriorating standards of living. N Nugent in an essay on 'Political Parties of the Far Right' in a book *The British Right*[18] published some years ago, reminded his readers that, 'Extreme right-wing movements have normally been successful in Western Europe when severe economic problems have become associated with other dislocating factors. This lesson of history should not be forgotten.'

References

1. The chronology was as follows: John Beane and Colin Jordan merged in February 1960 into the British National Party (BNP) with Andrew Fountaine as president. Colin Jordan created a uniformed cadre of the BNP called Spearhead which held summer camps with military training in 1960 and 1961. In February 1962 Colin Jordan backed by John Tyndall broke with Beane and Fountaine. And in July 1962 Colin Jordan held a rally in Trafalgar Square followed three weeks later by Oswald Mosley. Both ended in violence and arrests. (See Conflict studies No 92, July 1978, by Peter Shipley.) See also 'Spearhead' trial at the Old Bailey, October 1962.

2. *National Front,* Martin Walker, Fontana 1977.

3. In the *Exeter Weekly News,* 14 April 1978, David Holmes reported a military exercise in the Wild Life Park at Crediton near Exeter where rifles and revolvers were used. This exercise was worked out by John Banks who ran a mercenary recruiting agency in Camberley and who has, at various times, assembled groups of mercenaries for missions in Angola, Zaire, the West Indies and Rhodesia. The British Movement was to receive a commission for trained mercenaries recruited through the organization.

4. Anthony Hancock had South African investments — a bankers letter showing a receipt of R7,990 in February is reproduced in *Searchlight,* No 24, p 40.

5. See *Daily Express* exposé 17 June 1977, 'Secret of a house called Heidelberg'.

6. As stated on the literature it produces, available from Edward Budden, 35 Hollingbury Road, Brighton.

7. BM Wessex, London WC1V 6XX.

8. Paper, 'Survival and Revival of Fringe Christian Racist Groups' by the Rev K Leech.

9. Undated reference from article 'Problems of Race' in parish magazine, Burghfield Rectory near Reading.

10. *New African,* November 1978, contained Investigative Report by Victor Ndovi. On June 13, 1978, 13 British missionaries at Elim in eastern Rhodesia near the Mozambique frontier were brutally murdered. Pictures of the massacre horrified world opinion and a mood akin to hysteria gripped the British press. Some 80 Conservative MPs signed a motion demanding lifting of sanctions and recognition of the internal settlement.

    Mugabe and other ZAPU leaders denied responsibility for the Elim killings. They were in fact on very good terms with the missionaries. Their view is that the Selous Scouts killed the missionaries, firstly because they were suspected of being friendly with the nationalists, secondly because an atrocity which could be blamed on the guerrillas at a time when Smith was seeking international support for the internal settlement was a bonus.

    A few days earlier Rhodesian security forces had raided into Mozambique killing 17 African refugees and two Belgian missionaries.

    A 25-year-old African who had served with the Scouts gave evidence to a team of lawyers from the US, Belgium and Britain, members of the International Association of Democratic Lawyers (IADL). The soldier named Flint told the lawyers how he took part in the Elim killing. He also claimed to have worked with white South African security men since he joined up in 1972. He spoke of other massacres in which he took part. Flint's story is supported by the Catholic Commission for Justice and Peace which has collected over the years much evidence of atrocities by Rhodesian Security Forces.

11. *Movement,* No 32, winter 1977, Student Christian Movement.

12. Published by Paddington Press, 1980.

13. *Morning Star*, 24 October 1975.

14. Michael Billig, *Fascists 1978*, Harcourt Brace Jovanovich 1978. Malcolm Goldsmith; *A Christian Looks at the NF 1978*, available from the Race Relations Unit of the British Council of Churches.

15. A letter from the NF is printed in the *Rand Daily Mail* of 16 September 1976 which includes this sentence: 'Of special interest to South Africans is our unconditional support of white civilization in South Africa and Rhodesia and our determined intent to rebuild strong ties with the White Commonwealth.'

16. The NF have compiled a register of mercenaries willing 'to give practical assistance'. *Morning Star*, 17 March 1976.

17. Michael Billig, op cit.

18. *The British Right* (ed R King and N Nugent), Saxon House, London 1977.

4. White Solidarity

The Christian League of Southern Africa: London 1977

November 1977 was a busy month for Graeham Blainey, the new young organizer for the Christian League of Southern Africa in London. First, there was a threatening storm in Parliament.

On 8 November, Peter Blaker, a Tory MP who had visited South Africa as a guest of the South African Foundation, asked a question in the House of Commons about Sir Harold Wilson's allegations against MI5 and the claim by Chapman Pincher in the *Daily Express* 24 August 1977 that listening devices had been planted in No 10 Downing Street. Although Blaker was needling Sir Harold by asking his question, the South Africans could be expected to watch carefully in case the cat jumped out of the bag. *The Times* 9 November 1977 reported that the allegations included one that MI5 was incompetent and politically biased. Blaker told the House that the newspapers had reported Sir Harold as saying that the head of MI5 had told him there was a disaffected faction of extreme right-wing views inside the service and that he (Sir Harold) believed the service contained a faction sympathetic to the Rhodesian and South African authorities. Blaker, in the knowledge that the new PM, James Callaghan, thought the allegation ridiculous, hoped Sir Harold would find some opportunity to come to the House and make a full statement.[1] As far as the South Africans were concerned the less that was said the better.

On the evening of 9 November 1977, the annual dinner of the Anglo-Rhodesian Society took place, providing a special opportunity for meeting members of this hard-core body of absentee planters and supporters of Ian Smith and of canvassing support for two important CLSA events.[2] The first was the unofficial ceremony and service at the Cenotaph in Whitehall on Remembrance Day, in memory of those who had fallen in defence of 'white Christian civilization' in southern Africa. It was being jointly sponsored by the Anglo-Rhodesian Society,

67

the CLSA and the Anti-Communist League. The second event was a march to Downing Street on 26 November 1977, organized by the same bodies in protest at the proposed terms of the Anglo-American settlement which was then under intense negotiation. Blainey's job in relation to these two events was to make personal contacts, distribute pamphlets, organize advertisements and get some editorial pieces in the press. In this he was helped, as always, by the special information officers in the South African Embassy whose job was to keep a detailed information system on all possible sympathetic contacts.

For supporters of Rhodesia's illegal white rulers, there was a choice of two similar and equally unofficial events at the Cenotaph on Remembrance Day. The biggest was the annual National Front march and wreath laying, one of the most important events in the National Front calendar for which they demanded 'a massive manifestation of White solidarity'.[3] There was also the lower key and more respectable Anglo-Rhodesian affairs in which people like Lord Salisbury would walk. The organizers tried to keep the two distinct but the rank and file were not selective. There were jackboots in both marches. When it suited them, some members of the Anglo-Rhodesian Society and their co-sponsors sought National Front help to swell numbers.

In the event which the CLSA was promoting, there was a brass band and some 400 people took part. Wreaths were laid by Lt-Colonel 'Mad Mitch' Mitchell and David Lardner Burke, Chairman of the Anglo-Rhodesian Society, whose father was Minister of Law and Order in Ian Smith's régime and a hard-line supporter of white supremacy in Rhodesia.

The National Front march attracted an estimated 4,000 as it moved up from Victoria Station. John Tyndall laid a wreath, and on Monday, 14 November 1977, *The Times* carried the National Front story and ignored the Anglo-Rhodesians. In the Rhodesian papers the reverse was the case. The Rhodesian event was headline news and treated at length. On the same day, some newspapers reported that it was the first day of the Steve Biko inquest in Johannesburg. Peter Simple of the *Daily Telegraph*, 23 November 1977, wrote that it was 'a march in a good cause against what can truly be called the evil powers of this world'

. . . 'organized by the Christian League of Southern Africa and the Anti-Communist movement'. 'Great is the truth and shall prevail', he added.

In the CLSA's handbill to tout for marchers it said, 'Show the world via the international cameras that there is a big difference between the British Government and the British people and that Rhodesia does have friends.'

One of the means used to recruit support for this march was revealed in a letter to the Rhodesian *Sunday Mail*, 4 December 1977, from the chairman of a newly set up extremist group called BRAG — the British Rhodesian Action Group. It advertized for the first time in the November issue of the *Rhodesian Patriot*, a short-lived magazine supporting white government in Rhodesia . . . 'with the full support of the National Front, the most influential British organization determined to restore Britain as a White nation'. The letter told how Wynn, the chairman of BRAG, had been at a meeting of the Anglo-Rhodesian Society where 'a man from the Anti-Communist League was giving out his leaflets about the march'. This was Roy Dovaston, a right-wing businessman from Ware who returned from South Africa in 1975 and was briefly involved in recruiting mercenaries for Rhodesia. The 'Support Rhodesia march' leaflet, jointly sponsored by CLSA and the Anti-Communism Movement was printed by VCP (see page 92). The letter continues that this man was invited to attend a meeting in the Central Hall, Westminster in November 1977 where BRAG was being formed.

'A large number of those present were members of the NF and at this meeting the Anti-Communist man asked the NF people if they could supply enough stewards and persons to come along to the march as he didn't think enough people would turn up. The people present were only too pleased to help out. This same man went along to a meeting of the League of St George. At this meeting he gave out his leaflets about the march.'

In the Rhodesian *Sunday Mail* of 27 November 1977 it was reported that the march was made more notable by the large proportion of National Front supporters, dressed in combat uniforms, who joined the march, and handed out pamphlets and newsheets along the way. It continued:

'Several times Rhodesian supporters were called to curb the national Front anti-black jeering and Nazi salutes and, at one point in the march, a group of moderate National Front supporters moved in to block off from Press cameras one of the marchers who was dressed in jackboots and SS officer's cavalry breeches.'

Referring to the same events six months later in a letter to the

Guardian, 22 June 1978, Graeham Blainey wrote that the Christian League had never marched with the National Front and had not (yet) laid a wreath at the Cenotaph.

November 1977 was also the month when the British churches issued at least three major statements attacking racism. These statements were from the British Council of Churches, the Church of Scotland and the Roman Catholic Church. All condemned racism in direct terms.

How the Christian League works in South Africa

According to the *Pretoria News* 6 November 1978 'the actual organization of the League is fairly extensive. The central office in Church Street East is manned by seven full-time employees'. It has branch or regional offices in southern Africa, London, Basle in Switzerland and representatives in many other countries. The chairman and founder is the Rev Fred Shaw, a Methodist minister.

Shaw founded the CLSA in 1974 as a one-man band. None of the main English-speaking church denominations would have anything to do with him, but nevertheless the CLSA grew and appeared to have strong financial backing. Although the churches and the press have repeatedly challenged Shaw to tell the world where his money comes from, he has been notably reluctant to do so.

According to a feature in the League's own newspaper (*Encounter*, July 1978) the organization was then involved in some 17 projects which included:

- The publication of *Encounter* newspaper;
- The publication of a German language periodical (*Vox Africana*);
- Regional offices in Southern Africa, London, and soon in Washington as well;
- The promotion of an alternative theological seminary for those in training for the ministry;
- The establishment of a bookshop specializing in literature which can inform and educate Christians concerning present-day tendencies and evils;
- The formation of an international and national network whereby all Christian groups and individuals concerned about persecution and the dangers of communism may achieve a degree of solidarity;
- An educational programme to churches in other countries where the truth has been perverted concerning the true situation in Africa today;
- Assistance to those seeking theological and biblical training in

certain of our African townships;
— The Rhodesia Christian Group which is amalgamated with the CLSA.

Reports in South African newspapers and elsewhere have linked the League with the Information Department scandal. While the officers of the League have continued to deny the connection, the evidence has demonstrated the contrary (see Chapter 5).

Already in 1977, before the Information Department scandal broke, the Conference of the Methodist Church of Southern Africa had appointed a committee, under the chairmanship of the Rev H Kirkby, to investigate the League to determine 'whether it had a role to play in the proclamation of the Gospel of Christ'.[4] As a result of this committee's report the 1978 Conference of Methodist Churches in South Africa repudiated the Christian League and called on its members to do so as well. Questions of finance had played a very minor role in the consultation between the two organizations, the main difference being rooted in theology and policy. The text of the report, with its extensive quotations from members of the CLSA, provides one of the clearer accounts of what the CLSA believes, at least within the southern Africa context.[5]

Summary of Report of Methodist Church Committee Consultation with CLSA[6]

According to Fred Shaw, the CLSA began as a result of concern expressed by members of various 'mainline denominations' who felt their 'hands to be contaminated with blood'. This, he maintained, 'was due to the theological justification of violence and terror within our churches and the tendency of synods to regard doctrinal matters as trivial in relation to such matters as the affirmation of the WCC support for black liberation organizations and "terrorism".'

The CLSA existed to recall churches to 'the faith once delivered to the saints'. It is concerned that 'churches are in fact ministering to the lusts of men — not the common man, but those men hungry for power, and all this is done in the name of championing the cause of the poor.'

One of the CLSA's foremost aims, says Shaw, 'is to influence all churches to withdraw and disassociate themselves from the WCC and the SACC — seen to be a major source of ungodly doctrine and action infiltering (sic) the churches.'

'The CLSA's explicit doctrinal position is stated in its

71

constitution: "The League believes in the Holy Scriptures as the Word of God and accepts the Nicene Creed as its statement of faith." It associates itself with the Berlin Declaration on Ecumenism and the theological thought of such theologians as Dr Peter Beyerhaus.' In general, 'CLSA regards itself as standing within the theological tradition of John Wesley.'

The committee makes it clear that there were many points of interpretation in the understanding of an explicitly Methodist perspective with which it was in basic disagreement with the delegation from the CLSA.

One of the most important is that the CLSA is explicitly committed to confrontation with those theologies and organizations with which is it not in agreement. It opposes outright all those theologies included under the broad category of so-called 'humanism'. It wants to have all churches withdraw from the SACC and the WCC. But the Methodist tradition is one of consultation and dialogue, motivated to 'agree to disagree' if necessary but not to disassociate or condemn those who dare to express different theological opinion. Umbrella-type organizations such as the WCC or the SACC cannot be expected to affirm an homogeneous theological position, let alone a Methodist one. 'We have', say the committee, 'at no time questioned the Christian integrity with which their opinions are stated.' Dismissing 'those organizations and theological perspectives with which one cannot fully agree as "humanist" and "communist" influenced, is against the entire Methodist tradition.'

The committee saw the confrontation stance of the CLSA as 'based on a dogmatism rather than a careful assessment of the contemporary theological and social situation, leading to an unnecessary polarization of attitudes between Christians' which makes reconciliation difficult. The readiness of the CLSA to label those with whom it disagrees as Marxist, Freudian and the Anti-Christ was noted, while the CLSA saw its own position as biblical and of God. The CLSA delegation were prepared to regard their organization as containing 'all the truth' with regard to the proclamation of the gospel in all its dimensions.

Another way in which the CLSA polarized matters was its habit of gross over-simplification of the facts in attributing 'terrorism' to WCC support and black dissatisfaction and 'rioting' to communist agitation.

The report states: 'The CLSA does not share the committee's feeling that in this transitional period of history in which we live it is not always clear as to what God's will for His church is. Dogmatism and absolute certainty is regarded by the CLSA as a clear biblical requirement in regard to the truth and non-truth and this *organization has apparently little difficulty in knowing exactly what this socio-political or non-truth is*. While various organizations and churches are seen by the CLSA to view socio-political events from an ideological perspective they regard themselves as being non-ideologically determined and solely biblical in their assessment.'

'This position tends to foreclose debate, hardens attitudes and is not conducive to dialogue and reconciliation', the report concludes.

The committee found the CLSA not only under the influence of European theological thought, but on the whole unwilling to see the difference between the situation in western Europe and Britain and that in South Africa.

'The ecumenism debate in Europe', it felt, 'is of little direct relevance to the Southern African scene.' The committee did not feel that the CLSA was prepared to listen to 'the conflicting voices of our people'. It sensed 'a lack of real consultation with Blacks and a failure by the CLSA to reflect Black opinions at policy and self-identity level'. Despite the presence of five black representatives of the CLSA, the committee found what it called 'a singular lack of commitment by the CLSA to articulate legitimate Black grievances and aspirations'. One black minister on the committee felt that the CLSA was essentially a white organization.

It followed that the CLSA tended to be supportive of the *status quo* in South Africa, and that it was unprepared to attack apartheid. '*While the CLSA is prepared*', the report says, '*to unequivocally dismiss the WCC together with its ideals as the Anti-Christ*, in response to an explicit question, *it is not prepared to say apartheid is contrary to the scriptures and to be condemned by the Christian Church*. Neither is the CLSA prepared to say colonialism, imperialism or apartheid and *other forms of white racism are underlying contributory factors to the bloodshed that is dominant in Southern Africa today*.[7] The WCC is however seen to be responsible for a significant share of the bloodshed in Angola and Mozambique. The committee continually notes double standards being manifest in this regard by CLSA.'

The committee felt it would be impossible to continue membership with the WCC and the SACC and at the same time affirm the CLSA.

A discussion of CLSA's official newspaper *Encounter* found little common ground between the committee of the Methodist Church of South Africa and the CLSA. 'The CLSA delegation was not prepared to accept a suggestion that *Encounter* was given to irresponsible reporting and character assassination,' or that its 'articles had regularly failed to differentiate between facts on the one hand and comment on the other, as well as having tended to make a selective use of truth and half truth to promote a slanted interpretation of events.'

The committee was also critical of the CLSA's methods of attempting to influence and persuade 'the attitudes and opinions of members of local congregations at times without the prior consultation or permission of the minister concerned.' The Rev Shaw felt that if this were the case the discipline of the Methodist Church was adequate to deal with him. At one stage of the discussion he said 'that he never urged people not to support financially the work of the church' but later he admitted that 'there may have been occasions when he did in fact say such things openly'. The committee reported their grave misgivings about the whole matter. At their annual conference in 1978, the Methodist Church of Southern Africa accepted this report and gave a cold shoulder to the League in a motion which said: 'We cannot commend the CLSA to our people at this time.'

It was stated in the discussion, according to the South African *Daily Despatch*, 27 October 1978, that financial statements of the CLSA newspaper, *Encounter*, were not made available to the Methodist committee drawing up the report on the CLSA, on the grounds that the newspaper existed independently of the CLSA. It was, however, reported, the paper went on, that *Encounter* was financed, at least in part, by an American businessman.

Encounter, Official Newspaper of the Christian League of Southern Africa and the Rhodesian Christian Group

Encounter began publication in November 1975 as an eight-page monthly tabloid with an occasional supplement to include some particularly meaty matter which could not be accommodated in the normal run. An admitted 21,000 copies of *Encounter* are printed in South Africa for circulation there and abroad. Several thousand copies are sent by KLM to Holland from where they are airmailed to subscribers and in batches to representatives in different European countries (see Chapter

6). Graeham Blainey, the full-time London representative, says that 'several hundred *Encounters* are sent to me each month from South Africa, which I do my best to distribute promotionally, plus several thousand are sent direct . . .'

An analysis of the contents of *Encounter*, as an example of how it functions as a mouthpiece of the CLSA is instructive, both about the editorial policy of the paper and about the operations of the CLSA. The author is indebted to a South African Methodist minister (who cannot be named) for many of these insights.

First are examples of the remarkable support *Encounter* gives to the National Party of South Africa, and its apartheid policies.

1. Although *Encounter* does not offer regular book reviews, it invited readers to obtain from its book-store a much praised publication of the South African Freedom Association. It has since been revealed that the Foundation was a front organization financed by the secret funds of the Government's Department of Information and established to sell apartheid.

2. *Encounter* sought to defend the dealings of the discredited Department of Information and its misappropriation of funds by quoting approvingly from a South African journal *To the Point*, and the writings of Ivor Benson. *To the Point* is a pro-government publication edited by Dr Poorter, a former information officer of the South African Government in London. Benson was for a lengthy period compiler of the 'White South Africa Right or Wrong' propaganda programme broadcast by government-controlled radio and entitled Current Affairs.

3. At a time when the President of the Methodist Church in South Africa was referring to the uprooting of squatter families at Crossroads[8] (near Cape Town) as 'alien to every tenet of Christian justice and mercy', *Encounter* chose to see the world-wide concern as a deliberate attempt to provoke violence by those not caring for the wellbeing of people; these 'sympathisers being glad when people are hurt and killed in clashes with the police which they provoke'.

4. When *Encounter* was faced with the dilemma of responding to the death in detention of Steve Biko, it chose to

ignore the implications of this evil for both the Security Police and the system of detention without trial, and attributed his death to those who had been Biko's colleagues in the Christian Institute: 'They would do better now to remove their guilt of Steve Biko's death by seeking God's forgiveness for having failed to impart to him a faith in the God and Father of our Lord Jesus Christ.'

5. When *Encounter* wished to offer an interpretation of Black thinking in South Africa it quoted *Die Hervormer*, the official organ of a denomination which debars Blacks from membership: 'Nowhere in Africa do Black people appear as happy as our Blacks ... what happened in Soweto during 1976 and consequently leading to bloodshed was not a peaceful plea for reconciliation. It was brutal, provocative, instigated violence, arson and vandalism by agitators.'

The most disturbing aspect of the League's defence of the National Party and apartheid is that it calls darkness, light. *Encounter* seeks to justify the killing of children in Soweto and of Steve Biko in detention; homes bulldozed and families broken at Crossroads; theft of public funds and the clandestine operation of 'disinformation' agencies by the Department of Information.

The Working of the London Office of CLSA

In Britain the well-organized protest movements, the information gathering of a free press, the official position of the churches and of the mainline political parties present a challenge to any South African organization wanting to present a convincing case for the apartheid system. It was not enough that CLSA should hit out at 'liberal' church bodies within South Africa, it had to get at the sources of support, to stop the flow of monetary and other help from outside South Africa — much of this was from Britain.

In 1977 it launched a new programme of activities abroad. In July of that year CLSA's newspaper *Encounter* carried this piece:

BREAKTHROUGH IN BRITAIN

'The need to get the truth about Southern Africa across in Britain, and especially to British Christians, grows daily.

'Every effort to suppress the truth and destroy bridges of understanding is made by the British Foreign Office. Naked hostility marks much of the press, while the ecclesiastical closed mind reigns in most of the Churches and religious opinion-forming bodies. Prominent Rhodesians of British birth are refused entry to the country . . . Rhodesian advertisements are illegal.

'Yet thousands — maybe millions — want the truth about South Africa and Rhodesia.

How to break down the barrier?

LONDON OFFICE

'The CLSA is to open an office in London through which literature will be distributed and contacts made. Discreet but growing publicity will enable fairminded Britons to find the facts and to know where to turn to learn Southern African Christian opinion, that is, not the prefabricated product mass-produced and circulated with alien funds by the WCC and its fellow-travellers in Southern Africa.

Encounter will be distributed from this office.

'Mr Graeham Blainey has offered to run the office, and is straining at the leash to get going. He and his wife are both committed Christians, undertaking the job at considerable personal sacrifice. Pray for them in their new venture for Christ and for truth.

'The office address is: Christian League of Southern Africa, PO Box 8959, London WC1V 6XX.'

The article concluded by referring to contact with the Christian Affirmation Campaign and the British representative of the Rhodesia Christian Group and describing how the circulation of information would grow rapidly.

The office is on the sixth floor of an old block which also houses the Monday Club. In the best traditions of security, the front door carries no identification, but the interior boasts two telex machines, and other hardware. CLSA thrives on handling information, and on seizing the passing moment.

Blainey has certainly managed this and a good deal more. He has proved himself a tireless legman in the cause. With his earnest good looks and preference for polo-necked sweaters and slacks he gives the impression of being a pleasant and sincere young Christian from the Festival of Light or one of the evangelical sects. This impression is maintained when he is involved in discussion about the political role of the Christian League, but he becomes ill at ease and inarticulate in debate with anyone who is at home in the subject and gives a strong impression of someone caught up in matters he hardly understands. He works best with the prepared statement and the letter to the press or in the anonymous role of giving out leaflets.

The leaflets used are of two types — those designed to shock and those designed to provide some simple 'corrective' information about southern Africa. The photos appear to be taken from *The Citizen*, the government-financed newspaper. The pamphlets are printed in London.

Blainey himself distributes pamphlets by hand. These have been sighted around the Houses of Parliament, in Belgravia, Kensington and other parts of London. Blainey even picketed the 1978 Lambeth Conference at Canterbury, giving the bishops a leaflet condemning the World Council of Churches for helping 'terrorists' and even got one into the hands of the Archbishop of Canterbury.

The same all-purpose leaflets are also circulated with mailings from CLSA, and from various friendly or affiliated organizations such as the Christian Affirmation Campaign, the Anglo-Rhodesian Society, the Friends of Rhodesia, and by the efforts of individual members or supporters around the country. They have been dropped into the back rows of church pews, stuck on noticeboards, left under wipers on windscreens. They are also scattered on the table in the reception area of the Monday Club office.

Blainey's own report to Pretoria boasts that 'the leaflet distribution has really got under way now, with interested and concerned people writing in for bulk supplies of literature, very often including donations . . . [During the last month] many thousands were spoken to through the leaflets that were handed out as we "marched" through the heart of the packed-out West End of London.'[8]

It is difficult to estimate the number of leaflets which have been distributed. Whatever one's opinion about content, the quality is good — high gloss art paper or coloured cartridge. An estimated 20,000 of each of the three examples reproduced here would disappear rapidly and the actual printing figure may be a lot higher. Obviously cost in the last two years (1978 and 1979) has not been a problem.

In 1979 a pamphlet attacking Christian Aid was circulated

Bernard Smith (top left), Secretary of the Christian Affirmation Campaign, author of *The Fraudulent Gospel*. David Martin (top right), secretary of the British League of Rights etc.

Dr Peter Beyerhaus (left), German theologian and chairman of the International Christian Network. The Reverend Fred Shaw (right), chairman of the Christian League of Southern Africa.

HAS
CHRISTIAN AID
HELPED TERRORISTS?

YES

Like the World Council of Churches, Christian Aid has made gifts to the anti- Rhodesian terrorist groups of ZAPU and ZANU. They have also sent substantial aid to SWAPO.

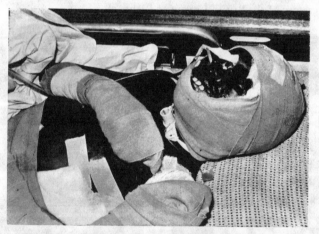

KANDO AMWEELO—Hurt in a Landmine explosion in Ovambo (South West Africa) in July 1977.

Stop Aid to Terrorists

Christian League of Southern Africa
Box 8959
London, WCIV 6XX

VCP LONDON WC2

Leaflet which was found in British churches in May 1979 just before Christian Aid Week.

A typical CLSA leaflet against the World Council of Churches, one of several distributed in the United Kingdom.

Bernard Smith at CAC Conference, 1979 with panel of speakers.

A 'mass' demonstration by CLSA supporters for the Lancaster House Constitutional Talks. Graham Blainey in centre.

TERRORISM
Helped by the World Council of Churches

RHODESIA

On July 15 1977, a group of terrorists entered a village in the Rushinga area, East of Mt. Darwin. An entire family—23 men, women, children and babies——were first beaten, and then herded into a hut which was subsequently set on fire. There were no survivors.

STOP AID TO TERRORISTS

Christian League of Southern Africa
BOX 8959, LONDON, WC1V 6XX

VCP London WC2

in the weeks prior to the charity's main funding week, in an obvious attempt to disrupt the charity's fund-raising efforts. It accused Christian Aid directly of helping 'terrorists' by making gifts to Zapu and Zanu, linking such help with the World Council of Churches' Programme to Combat Racism grants to liberation movements. Several British newsapers took up and echoed the allegation. The Director of Christian Aid's correspond-ence from dismayed supporters rose considerably. The accusation was untrue and public apologies and legal costs were obtained from the press.[10]

All printing is done by VCP — V Cooper and Partners, 6 Flitcroft Street, London WC2. They are also the printers for the Wessex Study Group, a nationalist and anti-immigrant cell offering literature anonymously. It is not known who their backer is.

At least 11 leaflets were produced during 1978 and 1979. Some contain more text than the two examples and have neither slogans nor photographs, but the themes are basically the same. The latest one attacks the Church of England General Synod for its grants to the CRRU. The CLSA call this 'defending the faith and putting out corrective information about conditions in southern Africa'. The British Council of Churches calls it 'racist propaganda of the most sensational . . . kind'.*

Another of Blainey's tasks is to organize and publicize platform events for the team of speakers from Pretoria. This is nearly always a matter of either 'hitching a lift' from some other body holding a regular meeting in which CLSA speakers might join, or organizing a joint event with a second or third sponsor. Fred Shaw has been a regular visitor at most CAC conferences. In September 1978 he was billed at a joint meeting with the Anglo-Rhodesian Society at Caxton hall on the Future of Southern Africa. Traditional Rhodesian lobby MPs Patrick Wall and Ronald Bell were also scheduled. 'Publicizing the presence of the two MPs should guarantee a substantial audience and good media coverage,'[11] wrote Blainey to Pretoria.

Unfortunately for the CLSA, what these two MPs have to say about the situation in southern Africa has been said by them over and over again in the same terms for years, a form of liturgy which neither the public nor the press find interesting.

Finding speaking engagements of any significance is a heavy task for Blainey. All the major denominations oppose the line taken by the CLSA and in those few pulpits where League members are welcome, they are more than likely speaking to a

---

* Since 1980 the CLSA output of leaflets has ceased, but a new version of its 'Red Herring? Nazism murdered 15 million people . . . Marxism has murdered 143 million etc.' has appeared in 1981, published by the Christian Affirmation Campaign but still using VCP, the CLSA's usual printer in Britain.

small band of the already converted.

It seemed like a breakthrough when Fred Shaw was invited to speak at Wesley House in Cambridge on 23 October 1978 on his return from the United States, and to give a sermon and address a meeting at St Andrews the Great in Cambridge, whose council had permitted resident South Africans to hold a regular service. 'So now we can make full use of the present opportunity,' wrote Shaw's correspondent in Cambridge. All the other churches and ecclesiastical establishments had declined to have Shaw. Despite eager bill-posting, contacts with the South African Embassy and even a call to Neede (a church in Holland which was trying to promote goodwill with the South African Government) to encourage attendance, Shaw's standard patter about the threat of communism in southern Africa and the British churches' help to 'terrorists' struck no responsive chord. At Wesley House there was a critical audience of nine. His reputation at Cambridge was not improved.

Another of Blainey's tasks was to monitor public meetings and conferences at which southern African affairs might be discussed and to report on what was said and by whom. When Bishop Desmond Tutu, the General Secretary of the South African Council of Churches, addressed a lunchtime meeting of the Royal Africa Society on 20 July 1978, Blainey was there. Tutu spoke of the growing tragedy of the confrontation between races in South Africa and talked of the need for a Christian presence in a situation of crisis. He was deeply critical of the present government in South Africa, but he spoke as a South African with a deep love of his country and a belief in its future. He deplored the lack of dialogue between black community organizations and government over new laws speeding up separate development (apartheid) which forced people towards a violent opposition. He spoke of the role of the Christian churches as a last chance in seeking a peaceful solution to South Africa's problems. Blainey reported that Tutu had supported disinvestment and that he had made a sinister remark: 'When we come to power we will remember who our friends are.'[12]

'Our concern is for people, not political systems or ideologies,' wrote Blainey in a letter to the *Guardian* 22 June 1978. But most of what he and his colleagues in the CLSA do has political and ideological consequences. The fact is inescapable.

On 28 August 1979, Bishop Tutu, who was again in London

on a brief visit, was taken to a meeting with the Evangelical Alliance who were interested to hear more about the recent SACLA meeting in South Africa and the SACC part in it.[13] They had also invited Graeham Blainey to attend. In a part of the discussion dealing with university education, Blainey made the statement that 50 per cent of the students admitted to Witwatersrand University that year were black. In this case Bishop Tutu was there to refute such misinformation. On the 28 July 1979 the Chancellor of the University, interviewed for the *Guardian* said, 'Last year about seven per cent of our 11,750 students were black, but each one needed special ministerial permission to come here.' According to the same article, there are 110,000 white students in South Africa, while three black universities, Fort Hare, Zululand, and the University of the North, muster a total of 6,000. The total number of black university students (including coloured) in South Africa is estimated at some 8,000 — that is a maximum of 13.7 per cent.

On this occasion it was possible to challenge an inaccurate statement directly and authoritatively, but there are many occasions when the facts of the official white South African view of apartheid are allowed to pass unquestioned. The representatives of the CLSA are just one of the many channels to the outside world which are thus used by the system.

This is how Blainey sees the objectives of the London office when summarizing it for his boss, not for the public, in a report which has come into our hands from a sensitive and highly reliable source: 'The London office has specifically been concentrating on putting out corrective information about conditions in southern Africa, which have been grossly misreported in the British Press. This false reporting builds up . . . and establishes the emotional climate wherein, for instance, the British Government can condone murderers such as Mugabe and Nkomo.' Or take the list of methods and activities which he uses as a guideline:

1. Widespread literature (leaflet distribution).
2. Contacting and 'working on' the media.
3. Petitioning and lobbying Parliament, the Foreign Office, etc.
4. Organizing various forms of public demonstration such as marches, vigils, etc.
5. Building contacts with, and working through, other

organizations such as the Young Conservatives etc.
6. Building up contacts with individuals such as MPs and sympathetic journalists.
7. Having available a library and booklist of good, relevant books.

These are the activities and methods of a political action group, confident and well organized, not that of an association of Christians whose main concern is a difference in view on Biblical truth and in the theology of salvation.

The main task of the CLSA has always been 'to ward off a Marxist black takeover in South Africa and to get churches to withdraw from both the World Council of Churches and the South African Council of Churches' (*Voice*, 11 November 1978).

Father Arthur Lewis and the Rhodesia Christian Group

Father Arthur Lewis, an Anglican priest and a senator in Ian Smith's Parliament, achieved the rare distinction in February 1979 of being barred by the Foreign Office from entering Britain, despite the fact that he was a British subject and had a British passport. For Lewis, it was just another step in his long march of increasingly bitter confrontation with the church leadership, with missionary colleagues, with the British Government and with a growing number of 'enemies' that were part of his own dark mythological world.

Father Lewis first went to Africa as a missionary in 1947 after reading theology at Oxford and being ordained as an Anglican priest in 1944. He worked successively in Zanzibar and in southern Tanzania (then Tanganyika) before moving to Rhodesia in 1958 with his wife Gladys, who was a trained nurse. They were on the face of it an ideal missionary team, but from the earliest days there seem to have been differences and difficulties both with the authorities and with community elements.

The span of Father Lewis's work in Africa from 1947 to the present day has seen great changes in Christian thinking towards missionary work. The important Church Assemblies of the 1960s and 1970s have reshaped worldwide 'joint actions' about communicating the gospel in a complex and changing world. It is a period when almost all the colonies within the Commonwealth gained their independence. All this time Father Lewis

was working, literally on the evangelical frontier, divorced from
the mainstream of the conferences and the new thinking. He
was, in all senses of the word, an old-fashioned missionary,
more at home with the concept of Africans as unruly and
sometimes disobedient children, than as equals in a new society.

One of Father Lewis's first tasks in Rhodesia was to make
something out of St Faith's Mission, the pioneering experiment
in racial equality built by Guy Clutton-Brock and dismantled
by the Southern Rhodesian Government. Lewis's experience in
bringing this former collective to heel was an unhappy one. He
wrote later that St Faith's made him 'completely determined
that St Peter's Mission, Mandea, shall be a mission in the true
sense, devoting itself to preaching the Gospel and to the conver-
sion and pastoral care of souls'. Lewis was at this time an
enthusiastic evangelical missionary. He was certainly not
racist, as is shown by his long commitment to working among
Africans in remote districts and his learning several vernacular
languages. He was, and knew himself to be, a paternalist of the
old school, but justified himself by stating that it was demanded
of him. From his time at St Faith's onwards, he clashed more
and more with a generation of Africans influenced by the wind
of change; by the new political ideas; by the nationalist tide
moving inexorably towards a black majority rule deeply influenced
by what Lewis now saw as 'the advancing forces of godless
communism'.

In the early 1960s he moved to St Peter's Mission, Mandea,
a remote but lush mission on the eastern frontiers of Rhodesia
in the Honde valley, overlooking Mozambique. With great
energy he organized St Peter's into a strong pastoral mission
and used his flair for vivid journalism to attract widespread
public support for educational and medical projects from
churches, social groups and individuals in the United Kingdom
with whom he corresponded by means of regular newsletters.
These *Letters to Friends* soon became a platform for more
than news about the mission. They ranged ever more widely
over his own views on the political problems of Rhodesia and
became a forum for his own intimate difficulties with his
diocesan colleagues, with his missionary headquarters in
London and with the people of Honde. He was frequently, it
seemed, the victim of 'misunderstanding' and developed the
habit of seeking the intercession of his supporters or even the
press, directly over the heads of his local superiors.

It was at St Bartholomew's, Rusape, a small town parish to

which Father Lewis was transferred from St Peter's, that the Rhodesian Christian Group was launched. Here are Father Lewis's own words from one of his newsletters:

'It was at the beginning of 1972 that a number of concerned Christians approached me, on the basis of a few things that I had written, and suggested a group to resist leftist bias and anti-Rhodesian politicking within the leadership of Rhodesian churches. So the Rhodesian Christian Group was born . . . one of the earlier Christian bodies to expose the Marxist machinations of the WCC. Since then church leaders in Rhodesia have changed their tune dramatically and we have joined with Christian anti-communist groups throughout the world: especially with the Pretoria-based Christian League of Southern Africa. Our literature, countering the torrent of falsehood about Rhodesia in church publications, reaches major countries of the free world in various languages. The WCC is at last on the defensive and we can honestly claim to be playing a part in the battle for biblical Christianity!'

This was good recruiting stuff, but hardly the objective truth.

Since then Father Lewis has not only written his occasional *Letters to Friends* but a series of newsletters, articles and booklets for the RCG. The RCG remains however a group of some four or five persons of whom Lewis is the best known. Another fellow missionary, Father Gardiner, occasionally shares a byline or a platform with him. Despite all kinds of publicity and engineered controversial setpieces in the press and on TV in the last seven years, the RCG has achieved no significant support from the mainline denominational churches in Zimbabwe/Rhodesia.

In 1976 Lewis was elected to the Senate in Salisbury as a Christian Independent, an event which further alienated him from the church leadership within Rhodesia and from his supporting missionary society in Britain. Indeed, while he was in the Senate he was no longer deemed to be carrying out any of the terms of his mission, so his name was removed from the lists kept by the United Society for the Propagation of the Gospel, an event Lewis tried to turn into a major controversy. His concern to defend the Smith régime in Rhodesia and to speak as its representative whenever his visited Britain was at least partly responsible for the Foreign Office banning him in 1979. Now that he has no official status, he is once again free to come and go as he pleases. He has in fact chosen to move to South Africa 'to find friends for some of those whose circumstances compel them to leave Zimbabwe,' and 'to help save something of Africa from the Marxist takeover.'[14]

In 1978, St Peter's Mandea had to be abandoned because it was no longer defensible against the guerrilla incursions in that part of the exposed frontier. All the local Africans had long since been removed by Rhodesian security forces to 'protected villages' and so the work of the mission had been destroyed.

The Main Themes of Father Lewis

Until the 1980 elections Father Lewis maintained that Rhodesia and South Africa were holding the front line for Christianity. The churches elsewhere had been subverted. 'We, in Rhodesia, with all our faults, stand for the Christian standards and civilization of the West,' or again, '. . . we are determined to defend the standards of Christian civilization against the flood of returning barbarians.' Now only South Africa holds the line.

Another theme is that of 'terrorism'. Father Lewis is involved in a personal crusade against 'terrorism', using his journalistic skill for graphic and gruesome description of atrocities, pain and grief. The churches are tainted by Marxism he says, and openly encourage 'the tactics of terrorism'. 'Through the World Council of Churches and its ancillaries, terror has been given the stamp of respectability.' *Christian Terror* is one of his recent booklets, a series of bloodthirsty accusations written at the pitch of an almost continuous scream.

A third theme is the world conspiracy. In the case of Father Lewis the main ingredient is not racism, but communism. He writes that he working 'against the rulers of darkness of this world'. The United Nations, for instance, is 'an embryonic quasi-Marxist world-government which can tell "sovereign" states what to do'.

The church has been hijacked 'by the political left . . . swept away in the red tide'.

'The true forces behind world-politics are hidden by a smoke-screen. American money and international finance feed Russians who can then arm and ferment war and revolution. The nature of the tie-up is a mystery to most of us but the arch-conspirator is Satan himself.' These and similar ideas have a long heritage amongst extreme right-wing political groups in many parts of the world and we shall look at them again later. The chairman of the Christian League of Southern Africa, the Rev Fred Shaw, holds similar views.

It is not surprising to find that soon after the formation of the CLSA in 1974 Father Lewis and Fred Shaw had become close collaborators, using each other's organizations and lists of supporters to spread their ideas more widely. Both parties gained by the relationship. Lewis, who remained denomination-ally isolated in Rhodesia, gained some Christian support from the backing of the Christian League and the possibility of a global platform for his testimony in *Encounter* and as a member of the CLSA's speakers' panel. The CLSA gained the services of a distinguished British missionary with front-line experience of 'terrorism' who shared the official South African line on holding the front for 'white Christian civilization'. His taste for lurid stories of African barbarities enlivened any platform and made good copy.

In Britain the RCG's occasional newsletters were circulated through the Christian Affirmation Campaign mailings and in generous reprints in *Encounter*. Father Lewis's articles appeared in the newsletter *On Target* for the British League of Rights, in *Housewives Today* for the Housewives League and in the magazine of the British Israel movement.

These are some of the more tangible enemies he attacks: the World Council of Churches, the Roman Catholic Church, the Society for the Propagation of the Gospel, the United Nations, the British Council of Churches, the All Africa Conference of Churches, the Christian Council of Rhodesia, plus a wide range of politicians.

Now that Father Lewis is no longer in the Rhodesian Senate and approaches retirement age, and Zimbabwe has a govern-ment which in his eyes represents 'evil' in a concentrated form, there is no further role for him in the country, nor can there be any role for any 'Christians' who echo his point of view. He will, for the moment, be welcome in South Africa where he can still find a ready audience, working closely with the CLSA.[15]

The Launching of the International Christian Network

In the early 1970s the work of the World Council of Churches was moving forward confidently. Each major conference seemed to bring fresh inspiration. The membership of all the largest Protestant confessions was assured. Of course there were plenty of problems and differences in the interpretation of new policies and new theological ideas designed to meet Christian needs in the fast-changing world of the last quarter of the twentieth century. At the same time there was confidence that all these problems could be met by the complex structures of consultation and committees which kept the staff of the World Council in touch with the world churches and their communities who provided the resources and strength of the continued ecumenical effort. Among the 420 million Christians estimated as the WCC membership there was a general unity of view.

Naturally there were and are pockets of dissent from the seemingly unstoppable march of ecumenism. Some critics in churches which belonged to the WCC believed in the efficacy of debate within the system. They might be concerned about the direction of one particular programme or theological innovation, but they preferred to work within and express their dissent rather than opt out. For them the total value of the work being undertaken far outweighed the scruples of a tiny minority. After all, the WCC never pretended to a homogeneous theological viewpoint. With so many different churches in loose contact, it was hardly imaginable.

Outside the Council there were some churches and a scattering of individuals within the main denominations who deeply opposed the direction in which Christianity and World Mission was being taken by the World Council of Churches. Given the right conditions, there was always the possibility that they might join together to form an opposition group.

The main opposition to the WCC is generally of the right and the violence with which the WCC is accused of being a Marxist front lends weight to this view. It does not follow, as some commentators have immediately inferred, that the WCC is a leftist body.

Any co-ordinated opposition to the WCC had to face two important contradictions. First, it is contradictory to oppose ecumenism in the churches on the grounds of its ecumenism, by setting up another sort of Christian ecumenical organisation to fight it. Second, it is a contradiction for anyone to deny the World Council the right to be political, because it is claimed that it is against the scriptures, and then to go about leading a world crusade against the subversion of Christian civilization by communism, or by involving oneself in a body whose objective is to attack the right of liberation movements to act against oppressive and even 'illegal' regimes.

In July 1975 Dr Carl McIntyre, the American president of an organization calling itself the International Council of Christian Churches (ICCC) was expelled from Kenya during a conference designed, it would seem, to upstage the World Council of Churches Assembly to be held in Nairobi later in the year. Dr McIntyre's inference that only white ruled states were capable of maintaining Christian civilization was made in independent Kenya where the growth of the church has been phenomenal in recent years.[16]

Carl McIntyre was well known in the States as a fundamentalist preacher who espoused right-wing political causes. After 1975 the ICCC has never again been a serious focus of opposition to the WCC, but even in old age McIntyre still campaigns and wields influence (see Chapter 7).

Berlin Declaration on Ecumenism

In Europe in the early 1970s there were various interconfessional consultations of traditional Christians looking for some kind of co-ordinated movement around which the standard of opposition to 'modernism' might be raised.[17] This movement became known as the *Berlin Declaration on Ecumenism* which took as a subtitle 'Freedom and Unity in Christ' which is confusingly like the slogan of the WCC's Assembly 'Jesus Christ Frees and Unites'.

One of the major figures around whom supporters rallied was the German theologian Dr Peter Beyerhaus, now Professor of Mission and Ecumenical Studies at Tübingen University. Beyerhaus was a fervent critic of the policies of the WCC and wrote several books on the subject: *Missions: Which Way?* (1971), *Shaken Foundations: Theological Foundation for Mission* (1972); *Bangkok 1973* (1974). He was a missionary in South Africa from 1957 to 1965 and is now an academic of some prestige. This prestige and his relative youth (51) made him a convincing potential leader.

Dr Beyerhaus was a frequent visitor to the meetings held in Britain by the Christian Affirmation Campaign and here he regularly met the Rev Fred Shaw, the Chairman of the Christian League of Southern Africa, and Father Arthur Lewis of the Rhodesia Christian Group.

A loose fellowship of these 'confessing' Christians existed in 1976 through 1978. Its members corresponded with each other, shared newsletters, published each other's articles, sought opportunities to promote themselves in the media, barking and biting at any opening provided by the 'enemy'. A loose network developed between clergymen and others in the 'white' Commonwealth, North America, Europe and southern Africa.

91

International Christian Network (ICN) Project

Of all the groups or individuals who made up this 'fellowship' it was the Christian League of Southern Africa which had the most muscle, professional organization, widest address lists, a generous travelling budget and apparently substantial financial resources. It also had the motive, indeed the need, to go 'international'. The CLSA found it impossible to mount a convincing campaign against the South African Council of Churches without directly attacking its overseas support. This support came from the main church denominations of the rich countries acting for the most part through the World Council of Churches. To turn off this tap, the CLSA needed to reach church membership in those rich countries, to persuade it that the CLSA view of its Christian duty was the right one and that the SACC and the WCC between them represented the anti-Christ. Furthermore, it was necessary that the mainspring of this campaign should not be seen as an exclusively pro-South African, pro-apartheid lobby. It needed a theological argument which could be maintained on general principles and not related solely to South African conditions. It also needed an issue which could be easily grasped and which would be of concern to the ordinary member of the community. The Berlin Declaration provided the first,* the issue of terrorism the second. As a bonus, terrorism could be equated with communism, and so anti-racism, Marxism and ecumenism could be spun together as parts of a single demonic threat. The strategy was simple. It might even be made to seem a spontaneous outburst of righteous indignation springing up all over the world.

Unfortunately, it did not work out quite as planned. In the July 1978 edition of *Encounter* the front page was devoted to an account of what the League is about, by its chairman the Rev Fred Shaw. In a section on 'What the Christian League is Doing' he wrote:

> 'The formation of an international and a national network whereby all Christian groups and individuals which are concerned about the persecution and dangers of communism may achieve a degree of solidarity.'

The same edition carried a news story announcing the troubled birth of just such a network. Headed 'SA Christian Group is Barred', it told of the refusal of the Methodist Church in London to allow the Westminster Central Hall to be used by 'a group of Christians planning to combat the Marxist leanings of

---

* Of the eight notables who signed the original Berlin Declaration giving addresses in South Africa, six are listed in the comprehensive membership charts of the Broederbond in Wilkins and Strydom's exposé of that organisation. (*The Broederbond*. Ivor Wilkins & Hans Strydom. Paddington Press Ltd. 1979).

the World Council of Churches'. The story continued, 'the group is the UK section of the Pretoria-based Christian League of Southern Africa who had planned a conference from July 4 to July 6'. The story was credited to *The Citizen*, the English-speaking South African newspaper secretly financed by the government. The reporter was John Jackson, who had links with certain information officers at the South African Embassy. Jackson spoke to Graeham Blainey, the CLSA's London representative, who told him that 'it was made clear to him that the meeting has been cancelled *because of the League's opposition to the WCC's pro-communist policies* [my italics].

But note the change of emphasis when the story is reported in the UK *Daily Telegraph*, 29 July 1978. Blainey specifically 'denied that the Conference of Confessing Christians supported apartheid, or was South African based. The movement started in West Germany', he said.

In May 1978, a couple of months before the conference, a document was prepared and circulated by the Christian League from their Pretoria office entitled: Project: International Network of Confessing Christians. It was a description of the proposed aims, methods and results of a hypothetical 'network' (see p 94). Each item in this document is full of interest, illustrating the methods of the Christian League. An example is reproduced below, and provides strong circumstantial evidence that it was the South Africans who were determined to turn a dream into a practical reality. Their confidence in being able to back it with resources is a determining factor in the launch of the organization. Whatever glosses or denials have been made since, the objective of the network was in fact the establishment of an effective alternative to the WCC.

Launch of the ICN in London

The planned London launch was not only marred by the last minute change of venue and, at best, sceptical press reports which preceded it. The organizers expected over a hundred delegates. In the event, the conference attracted about 42 persons and — it was noted — a fair number were either observers or members of the press. The *Guardian*, 5 July 1978, drew a parallel between the 40-odd delegates representing a tiny number elsewhere in the world, and the 420 million believers who gave their allegiance to the World Council of Churches, at

PROJECT
INTERNATIONAL NETWORK OF CONFESSING CHRISTIANS

Description

1. To form a network of confessing Christians within the mainline Churches and particularly of those whose denominations belong to the WCC.
2. To turn back the growing influence of Christo-Marxism within these churches.
3. To promote the views and warnings of many outstanding Theologians of world renown who are being systematically silenced.
4. To have an organisation countering the political activities of the WCC in regard to South Africa, Rhodesia, Taiwan and Chile.
5. To awaken the Western Christian world to the dangers of Black Theology.
6. To rally support for the persecuted church in Eastern Europe.
7. To create a degree of solidarity among concerned Churches who hold to the Historical Christian Faith.
8. To establish a directory giving names and addresses of all persons and individual churches in the western world who are in sympathy with us.

Method

1. To operate within the Fellowship of Confessing Christians in Western Germany.
2. To have meetings in London in July this year comprising the following plus others still to be contacted:
   a. Prof Peter Beyerhaus of Tubingen University
   b. Dr R Sauerzapf of Bonn
   c. Prof Wisloff of Sweden
   d. Rev M Calder of New Zealand
   e. Dr Robinson of Australia
   f. Dr Keysor — United Methodist of USA
   g. Representatives of: The Presbyterian Church of America
   h.   The New Episcopalian Church of America
   i.   The Episcopalian Church of America
   j. Representatives from the various churches in Canada still to be arranged
   k. The Presbyterian leaders of the Campaign for the Complete Withdrawal of the Church from the WCC in N Ireland.
   l. Representatives from all churches in Britain
   m. Representatives from the CLSA
   n. Representatives from the RCG
   o. Representatives from the CAC

Prof Beyerhaus will also obtain further names of theologians who are interested in Europe. Possibly 50 will attend.

Results:

Possible monthly newspaper and office in London with competent staff with financial support from all participating groups to maintain the same.

The establishment of an effectual alternative to the WCC.

which the ICN was tilting. The *Daily Telegraph*, 10 July 1978, called the conference 'a small but determined body'. Dr Beyer-haus, in a keynote speech, saw the work of Satan in the opposition to the conference. Only a few, he said, have not bowed the knee to Baal. 'We cannot create an alternative WCC but we can spread information about the dangers of modernism and false ecumenism. We can pray and we can provide occasions for meeting.'

The Rev David Kingdon was announced at the conference as the Baptist Principal of the Baptist College of Northern Ireland, although he had in fact resigned the post some years before and had only recently returned after four years in South Africa as a minister and staff member of the CLSA. He spoke about the theology of liberation against whose effects, he said, Rhodesia, South Africa and South West Africa were successfully defending themselves.

The Rev Fred Shaw, giving an exclusive interview in the *Daily Telegraph*, 13 July 1978, lambasted the World Council, saying it was full of 'misguided clerics', a 'committed band of deceived deceivers' he called them, and he pointed to the distribution of large sums to terrorists groups which are 'helping black people to be persuaded to overthrow Christianity and use violence to establish a Marxist regime.'

In November 1978 David Kingdon became the first executive secretary of the renamed International Christian Network with an office at 53 Victoria Street, Westminster. The first ICN newsletter announced an interim committee with Dr Peter Beyerhaus as Chairman, Dr Paul Mickey (USA) as Vice-Chairman, the Rev Maurice Cartledge (UK) as Recording Secretary, the Rev Fred Shaw as Regional Chairman for Southern Africa, the Rev Matthew Calder from New Zealand as Regional Chairman for Oceania. A further conference was announced to be held in late August 1979 in the USA. But there has been little public evidence of ICN activity during its first year of existence. In the first few months after the launch it must have become quite clear to the organizers that no major denominations either in Europe or elsewhere were going to join the ICN. Indeed, there was no breakthrough of any kind. Instead of the expected burst of recruiting activity, ICN has been a very low-key affair. More recently David Kingdon withdrew and accepted a Baptist pastorate in Cardigan. The conference in the USA was cancelled.

In early 1980 the CLSA tried to revive the flagging ICN through the purchase of the defunct *Christian World* in Britain and enliven it into an international Christian mouthpiece for its news.[18] In the summer of 1980, Dr John Mitchell, the former chairman of the CLSA's finance committee came to England from South Africa and went to live in Abingdon. He is listed on a recent ICN prospectus as its new exec secretary.

The mailing effort has been modest. Most of the work seems to have consisted of trying to infiltrate other church organizations such as the Evangelical Alliance. The scandal which broke around the South African Government at the end of 1978 in relation to the secret funding of propaganda projects overseas was a serious setback. A connection between the Christian League and the Department of Information has been repeatedly alleged by the press in different countries in the wake of official enquiries and as a result of the press interviews given by Dr Eschel Rhoodie. Any link has strongly been denied by the Chairman of the League. Nevertheless this connection must now be considered. The role of the ICN as the outreach programme of the CLSA has to be seen in this perspective.

References

1. *Daily Express*, 24 August 1977, 'Spies who failed Harold'.

2. The Anglo-Rhodesian Society's objectives were to explain Rhodesian peoples and its régime to Britain. In the mid-70s, the secretary Tom Lawler claimed a membership of 5,000 (*Rhodesian Herald* 6 December 1973) and that it organized cheap flights for people wanting to visit Rhodesia.

   In the *Guardian*, 20 August 1976, discussing how mercenaries reached Rhodesia, it was reported that many recruits might be using the London-based Anglo-Rhodesian Society. The general secretary Tom Lawler said, 'We have no way — or for that matter, any reason — for stopping them'. In the *Rhodesian Herald* of 5 March 1976 (during UDI) there was a news item about a number of pro-Rhodesian Government posters on display in Salisbury, believed to have been sent by supporters of the Anglo-Rhodesian Society, which claimed that Rhodesia had been betrayed by Britain. It was supposed to be part of a world-wide poster campaign. One poster said, 'We did not yield in the dark days of the 1940s when your people the Rhodesians fought with us against the enemy.'

3. *Spearhead*, October 1977.

4. Minutes of 1977 Conference of the Methodist Church of South Africa, p 191.

5. The consultation took place in July 1978.

6. Report of Committee appointed by the 1977 Conference to consult with the Christian League of Southern Africa and report back to 1978 Conference.

7. Italics from the report itself.

8. Crossroads is a squatters' camp outside Cape Town housing migrant workers and their families. Government attempts in 1978 to demolish the camp (in terms of the Illegal Squatting Act, under which three other such camps — at Modderdam, Werkgenot and Unibel — had been demolished in 1977 and 1978) were defeated by a national and international campaign conducted by the squatters and their supporters, particularly within the churches, both inside and outside South Africa.

9. Report of CLSA London office, 15 July 1978, to its headquarters in Pretoria.

10. There was no impact on Christian Aid's fund-raising effort which in 1979 rose to record heights.

11. Report of CLSA London office, 15 July 1978, to its headquarters in Pretoria.

12. Report of CLSA London office, 15 July 1978, to its headquarters in Pretoria.

13. SACLA, the South African Christian Leadership Assembly, Pretoria 5–15 July 1979, the largest inter-denominational and cross-cultural rally ever held in South Africa.

14. *Occasional Newsletter*, May 1980.

15. The Church Times 15 August 1980 carried a report headed 'Fr Lewis "stunned" by CLSA revelation'. In the latest occasional newsletter written by Father Lewis, he said that the revelation that the 'Christian League' had been secretly financed by the South African government came as a 'stunning blow'. He added: 'Since the Christian League is almost the only voice which has effectively challenged SACC thinking, it would be gratifying to report that its own record is above reproach. A Government Minister, however, has made it clear that Government money has in the past been covertly put into it: and a time must have been reached when this was known to the League itself.

'The news comes as a stunning blow to me personally and to the Rhodesia Christian Group. I imagine the same must be true of many in the League, whose executive was certainly ignorant of any such subsidy.'

16. *The Times*, 26 July 1975; *Methodist Recorder*, 14 August 1975.

17. See footnote in Chapter 2 for definition of 'modernism'.

18. Author's own enquiries and correspondence.

5. South Africa's Propaganda Machine and the Churches

The Background of the Grand Design

The churches were, and still are, a major target of South Africa's aggressive 'information' campaign. It is pertinent, therefore, to sketch an outline of the development of the known elements of this propaganda war in order to fit the churches' role into perspective.

A series of scandals of extravagance and mismanagement by high-ranking officials in the South African Government were exposed in the English-speaking South African press in spring 1978. The Department of Information's plan to improve South Africa's standing abroad was revealed as a grand design of secret projects funded by a secret G-fund, financed from a special account of the defence budget.

Dr Connie Mulder, Minister of Information at the time and tipped as Prime Minister Vorster's successor, was one of the three most powerful men in South Africa. The other two were the Prime Minister himself and General Van Den Bergh, head of the Bureau of State Security (BOSS). As the enquiry proceeded they were all revealed as being implicated in the allocation of secret funds to the Department of Information for use abroad and in South Africa itself. One by one they were forced to resign their office. First Connie Mulder, then General Van Den Bergh and finally Prime Minister Vorster.

Vorster had initially denied all knowledge of the plot both in Parliament and in public but finally, under increasing pressure, admitted on 8 July 1978 that he had known about the secret fund 'to assist in a delicate and unconventional way in combating the total onslaught of propaganda against South Africa'[1] since 1972.

The same enquiries had also precipitated the flight abroad into hiding of the State Secretary of the Department of Information, Dr Eschel Rhoodie, whose master-plan for a South African propaganda war was the cause of the turmoil.

Dr Rhoodie's flight was seen by his former colleagues not

only as a desire to escape their political wrath and the threat of personal violence against him in view of his damaging inside knowledge, but also as an escape from the legal consequences of the alleged misappropriation of part of the secret funds.

In South Africa itself, ponderous official enquiries, and the cautious but determined press (in view of censorship restrictions and the threat of a total press-gag), teased out more and more details of the clandestine activities of the Department of Information. Meanwhile Dr Rhoodie, moving from place to place, put together his own dossier of facts in the form of a well-publicized cache of 41 secret tapes containing more evidence of secret South African propaganda and secret security actions around the world to be released if any 'dirty trick' was attempted against him personally. At the same time he was attempting unsuccessfully to bargain for his freedom with the new government of Prime Minister P W Botha. In South Africa the disclosures ruined the careers of many government employees and created the worst crisis of the soul for Afrikaners in 30 years of Nationalist Party rule.

For the four million white minority of South Africans, Muldergate, as it became known, was to do with the survival of white supremacy. To the 23 million black South Africans it was a farce: the régime that kept them in the position of second-class citizens for many decades had once more exposed itself to world ridicule.

As the various interested parties manoeuvred for personal or political advantage in the widening scandal, Dr Rhoodie was arrested in France. His appeal against extradition failed and he was flown back to South Africa to face charges of fraud and theft.

Before he was flown back, Dr Rhoodie spoke at length to an old friend and colleague Dr Ferry Hoogendijk of the Dutch magazine *Elseviers*, who started a series of detailed interviews about aspects of the Grand Design which had not been admitted or authenticated. It is these interviews in particular which have highlighted the importance of that part of the propaganda war directed against the church in South Africa and against the World Council of Churches overseas. In particular, the interviews examined in some detail the part played by the Christian League of Southern Africa.

In October 1979, Dr Rhoodie was tried on various misappropriation charges, found guilty on charges involving £36,000 and given leave to appeal. Pending the appeal he was freed on bail and left in restricted liberty in South Africa.[*] Some of the monies involved have been recovered, but there is a widespread feeling amongst South Africa watchers that only the 'tip of the iceberg' has so far emerged. It is certainly true that many of the secret projects are being continued under the reconstructed information bureau in South Africa.

Rex Gibson, editor of the South African *Sunday Express*, during a three-day seminar on 'The Survival of the Press' in October 1979, told the mainly professional audience that the Rhoodie trial got nowhere near the heart of things and that we have not heard the full story about the Information scandal. He said 'We haven't seen the full evidence given to the Erasmus Commission. We don't know how that Commission arrived at its findings . . . We don't know whether some people have been made scapegoats and others allowed to go unscathed. And we don't know anything about the 50 or 60 projects from the bad old Information days which are still being carried on.'

The scandal has raised serious moral issues among Afrikaner nationalists about the virtue of clean government or the expediency of a ruthless policy of survival. These issues remain unresolved but there have been many signs that, after a ritual breast-beating, things will continue as before. The Nationalist Party is so deeply entrenched in South Africa and isolated in the world that even a scandal of such dimensions cannot move it.

The trial of Dr Rhoodie attempted to destroy his credibility. Whatever the truth of his alleged personal involvement in the mismanagement or misappropriation of secret funds, it does not necessarily destroy his evidence on political dealings. Dr Rhoodie's evidence about the actual mechanics of how the information policy was developed, has, in the main, been found to be correct. In many cases his evidence was at first denied by frightened project-holders whose secret work had been exposed. Only later did overwhelming proof force them to admit the cover-up. The model of all such activity is the CIA, as revealed in recent accounts. The extraordinary lengths to which this organization was able to go should give one pause for thought in probing the connections that could exist within international charitable or church organizations. There should be no relaxation of vigilance because of a successful attempt by the South Africans to make Dr Rhoodie a public scapegoat for the system. The subsequent exposure of a South African spy within the directorate of the International Universities Exchange Fund (IUEF) confirm many of one's worst and most

*See Reference 6 on p 20.

paranoid suspicions.[2]

Nor can murder be ruled out as a weapon if the system is threatened. The whole world was shocked at the way Steve Biko died in a South African prison as a result of police brutality and the deliberate withholding of medical help. Before his death and after, many less well known Africans died in mysterious circumstances while under interrogation by the South African police, but the assassination of a prominent Afrikaner politician, possibly to seal his mouth, was something new.

On the night of 22 November 1977, Robert Smit and his wife Jeanne-Cora were killed at their home at Selcourt near Springs, 25 miles east of Johannesburg, a week before the national elections in which Smit was a National Party candidate. The killers have never been traced. Jeanne-Cora was shot and stabbed 14 times. Robert Smit was also stabbed and shot three times. The killers sprayed six letters in red aerosol paint on the refrigerator and walls of the house. They spelt RAU and TEN. The motive for the killing was not robbery since the contents of the house were untouched. The South African papers speculated that there might be a political motive. It was indeed a model CIA-type assassination.

Robert Smit was 44 and a leading South African economist. He had a fine academic record and was strongly tipped as a future Finance Minister. He was at the time of his death South Africa's alternative director on the International Monetary Fund (IMF), a frequent visitor at the World Bank's headquarters in Washington DC, and the managing director of the giant Afrikaans company SANTAM International, one of South Africa's biggest financial and insurance conglomerates. An Oxford Rhodes scholar and widely travelled, Smit was a committed internationalist and one of the few Afrikaners able to bring a world vision to the South African predicament.

For months the investigations, led by Detective Gerrit Viljoen under the supervision of the chief of the South African CID, General Kobus Visser, failed to bear fruit. As the Muldergate scandal evolved during 1978, however, press speculation began to link the assassination with the cover-up. It was alleged that Smit had been murdered because he had uncovered secret South African funds in America and was about to inform a Cabinet Minister.

Speculation was renewed in early 1979 when a former South African judge, Mr Justice Joe Ludorf, told the press that a client of his, a retired airline pilot Captain Sidney Excell, had evidence that two men had flown from an airfield near Luton, England to Lanseria Airport near Pretoria on a secret mission to kill the Smits. Captain Excell further said that he believed the mysterious acronym RAU TEN was possibly connected with the name of a former German Congo mercenary who had been involved in other African coups (*Rand Daily Mail*, 18 February 1979).

On 24 February 1980, a further sensational chapter was added by Joe Tranto of the American *Sunday News Journal of Delaware* who, after a year of investigation, alleged that two Cuban professional 'hitmen' who had links with BOSS, the CIA and the Chilean secret service DINA, had killed the Smits. The story connected these men, Jode Suarez and Virgilio Paz, with at least a dozen international assassinations since 1974 and alleged that men were recruited with the help of agents 'for the South African and Chilean 'secret police'.[3]

The article put a figure of R58,330,000 on the South African slush fund in American banks. It also said that Smit had discovered, shortly before his death, the names of more than 20 American politicians — including US senators — right-wing journalists and publishers who had received pay-offs from the slush fund in exchange for opposing sanctions against South Africa for its apartheid policies. Some of these Americans had been strong supporters of General Pinochet's government in Chile. The South African Minister of Justice, Louis le Grange, predictably denied the existence of such a fund or such information being a possible motive for murder. General Visser and Detective Viljoen flew secretly to Britain on 20 January 1980 to link up with joint investigations by Scotland Yard's Special Crimes Squad and other European contacts. The South African press were asked to keep the visit secret so as not to jeopardize enquiries.

Within the orbit of the former Department of Information interests, the game of bluff still goes on, a game of denial, protestation of innocence, refusal to talk to journalists. When the evidence proves too strong to deny, sullen admission or recantation usually follows. Some of the secret organizations have succeeded, temporarily perhaps, in withdrawing from view until public interest wanes. Other organizations have been irrecoverably exposed. Their usefulness at an end, they have been terminated and dismantled.

In one of the earliest moves to earth the shock-waves of public disclosure, the notorious BOSS became DONS — Department of National Security — and in February 1980 the name was changed again to NIS — National Intelligence Service, its influential role apparently downgraded. The old South African Department of Information was dismantled and its best known officers dispersed or retired. But in its place sprang up the Bureau for National and International Communications and then in another metamorphosis it became the Information Service of South Africa — ISSA. It operates from the same old offices, with presumably the same files. Its annual budget may be reduced but it has been working hard to repair the damage of the Muldergate scandal on the image of South Africa abroad. The links with the information officers in South African Embassies around the world remain intact. As GPD Terblanche said in the South African Parliament:

'These people of ours fight in the front line for South Africa against fanatical militant groups, against hotbeds of leftist liberalism, against mass communications media and against Red onslaughts. They have to cope with a flood of anti-South African propaganda, with a campaign of suspicion mongering, of misrepresentation and condemnation. This small group, those 60 men of ours abroad, stand alone against forces of subversion and political terrorism; against double standards and against the lie. They stand like a David of old against Goliath in their fight for South Africa.'[4]

The role of the Information Departments in the South African Embassies has worried anti-apartheid organizations throughout Europe for some time and demands for enquiries have often been launched. It has long been clear that their role goes far beyond the mere giving and gathering of information. A strong case has more than once been made that embassy staff have directly interfered in the political affairs of the host country.

But at the same time as Terblanche was voicing the fear of the embattled Afrikaner, his country was in fact spending vast sums on advertising, publishing and promoting propaganda campaigns throughout the world. It had plans to subvert politicians by bribery and to interfere in the domestic affairs of many countries. It was buying its way into a worldwide mass communication network and had purchased a slice of several fanatical militant groups to work on its behalf.

As a former information officer, Dr Rhoodie knew from personal experience how to mobilize the resources of embassy staff. He was already in government service as counsellor in charge of information at the South African Embassy at the Hague when his book *The Paper Curtain* was published in 1969 in South Africa. The paper curtain of the title was the barrier which cut off information about any of South Africa's positive achievements from the news media of the world. In Rhoodie's view the news media were only interested in reporting riots and racial discrimination in South Africa. The book proposed a positive change of direction for South African information policy.

From the time of the killings at Sharpeville in 1960 onwards, it had seemed that South Africa was losing all its friends. Every day the fear of a total international trade sanction loomed larger and anyone with ideas of how to restore the country's good image abroad commanded attention.

Rhoodie was called back from Holland for a confidential chat with Dr Connie Mulder, the then Minister of Information, whose imagination was fired by *The Paper Curtain*. The Minister proposed that Rhoodie's wide experience during his 13 years in the information departments of South African embassies around the world be harnessed to a programme to develop a more aggressive information policy for his country. Within two years he had been promoted over the heads of many senior civil servants to the post of State Secretary of the Department of Information, in effect the executive director of that ministry.

The Department's 'visible' budget rose sharply. It had been some R5 million in 1968 and rose to R11.8 million by 1975 and up to R16 million in 1978. (The rand was valued at about 1.7 to the pound sterling.)

This was not all. There was also a massive campaign of 'undiplomatic diplomacy' launched with the help of a special secret fund to be financed via BOSS from a special fund of the defence budget which was approved by a committee of ministers but without parliamentary sanction or knowledge.

In February 1974 there was an historic secret meeting between the then Prime Minister John Vorster, the Minister of Information Dr Connie Mulder, the Minister of Finance Dr Nico Diederichs and BOSS chief General Van Den Bergh, to discuss the detailed proposals tabled by Dr Rhoodie and his two deputy secretaries Denys Rhoodie and Les de Villiers. These wide-ranging proposals were for a five-year 'Grand Design' with a special guaranteed budget of over £10 million a year (Rhoodie has said it was 50 million guilders which at the current rate of 4.5gs to the pound produces over £11 million). Rhoodie felt such a scheme could only succeed if it came from the secret funds available to the Ministry of Defence and was not subject to parliamentary approval or knowledge. The money was to finance covert projects of a sensitive or secret nature, including, if necessary, the large-scale bribery and corruption of officials, newspapermen, politicians, businessmen, academics and church leaders, to buy a better image for South Africa during the crucial years ahead — 'key years for South Africa and of decisive significance for the future of the country', Rhoodie told the Dutch magazine *Elseviers*.

In October 1974 Dr Connie Mulder said in the South African Parliament, 'I have said before that my department will not remain on the defensive — we have now gone over to the offensive.' In the same year the general strategy of the whole propaganda campaign was mapped out. Bypassing all democratic procedures, in a style more reminiscent of Britain's Charles I, a committee of three ministers was to be responsible for the general approval of the programme and its costs. Equally important, a clandestine method was evolved by which vast sums of money were to be employed in South Africa and in different parts of the world in a way that would ensure that the original sources of the money would not be detectable. This is known as 'laundering'.

A company called Thesaurus Continental Securities Corporation was set up as a subsidiary of the Union Bank of Switzerland in Zurich through which most of the money to finance overseas projects could be passed. The Union Bank was chosen because for many years it had been one of the principal European banks for the South African Rembrandt Tobacco Group which had strong links with the Nationalist Party. Its ex-Chairman Dr Nico Diederichs was then Finance Minister and had been one of the architects of the powerful Broederbond Movement. Dr Diederichs was also instrumental in securing the co-operation of many prominent business men in Department of Information projects. These businessmen were either used to set up deals which helped fulfil part of the master plan or as a way of 'laundering' money in the form of 'unsolicited' contributions to organizations which were brought into the network.

During one of the official investigations into the Department of Information, a report in the *Financial Times*, 4 November 1978, stated that Pieter Van Rooyen, a lawyer in South Africa who had been a police advocate at the Steve Biko trial, had said that 'finance was channelled from a Swiss company Thesaurus Continental Securities to his own 'front' company, Thor Communicators, before being passed on to

105

another bank account. Thesaurus, he believed, was a front company for the Bureau of State Security, used to disguise the source of funds and transfer them from one government department to another. In this way, he said, some US$5 million was channelled through Thor, although he was not at the time aware of its destination.

Another front company which used the same address as Thor was the Homerus Finance Corporation, one of whose directors was David Abramson, the chairman of the printing and publishing company Hortors, and one of the businessmen Dr Nico Diederichs engaged in order to promote an international pro-South African publishing empire. Millions of rands were passed through Homerus in the form of 'interest-free loans' to buy shares and help the efforts of Abramson and his colleague, Stuart Pegg, to gain control of a wide range of British and European publications.

The Pretorius Commission, one of the bodies set up to investigate the DOI in 1978, identified 138 secret projects. Of this number, 57 had already been terminated, 68 were to continue — 56 of them secretly — a further eight were to be openly financed and two were to be handed over to the Ministry of Foreign Affairs. This left a small number unaccounted for.

A number of the secret projects were aimed at Christian organizations opposed to apartheid. The system just outlined offered channels of sponsorship, and infiltration without the source of those funds being revealed. In some cases money was available without responsibility or accountability and therefore quite beyond investigation. The full picture may never be known.

At the same time many recipients of financial support had to be given the means of protecting their 'honesty' or 'integrity' by being able to dissemble the source of funding, rationalize it in some way, or at least turn the finger away from South African official sources. The generosity or apparent philanthropy of businessmen was one cover used by the Department of Information.

The American businessman and publisher John McGoff, a regular visitor to South Africa and a personal friend of many of its leaders, was one such businessman. He agreed to head a series of attempted business coups in North America, seen as a critical battlefield by the South Africans. One of these was an attempt to buy the *Washington Star* with the help of R10 million lent by the Department of Information through Thesaurus

Securities, but he also provided at least one plausible channel for the financing of the Christian League of Southern Africa by his 'generous' support of their *Encounter* newspaper (see page 112).

The Beleaguered Christians

Gaining support for South African government policies within the mainline Christian churches was an important objective for Dr Rhoodie and his colleagues.

One might pause and wonder why the churches should be considered important enough for the South African Government to be prepared to spend large sums of money infiltrating and subverting them by covert action? A brief answer is that despite years of surveillance and restriction, of bannings and laws designed to stifle criticism of apartheid, some churches still publicly oppose the system. The government 'which had God on its side' found the situation intolerable and longed to neutralize such Christian opposition.

The major church denominations in South Africa are joined together in the South African Council of Churches. This ecumenical organization of Christians stubbornly opposes the racist policies of the government; it maintains relentlessly that apartheid is evil and unbiblical; it fights the evil of migratory labour and reminds the Afrikaner that even the Dutch Reformed church has said that this practice is a 'cancer' in society; it condemns detention without trial and the abrogation of law. In a society increasingly polarized between white and black, it fights for equal rights but seeks to maintain the middle ground of dialogue.

While considerable financial backing comes from Christians within South Africa, the bulk of the finance for the SACC's wide range of church-sponsored humanitarian projects in the black community, social and educational work, medical centres and the support of families of detainees, comes from churches abroad. Much of this world-wide support is channelled by way of the World Council of Churches.

By its championship of the black majority in South Africa, the SACC with its worldwide denominational support is seen by some as undermining the economic foundations of apartheid. In recent years church bodies in Britain and in North America have launched disinvestment campaigns, the effectiveness of which is beginning to be noticeable and worrying for the white

107

business community. Black theology, with its message that God's first concern is for the poor and the oppressed, directly undermines the Afrikaner's divine mandate to rule South Africa.

Here was motive enough to justify almost any campaign to discredit the South African Council of Churches. For behind it are the main denominations and churches in South Africa and their leaders. Behind them again are the churches of the richest countries which support the World Council of Churches, their leaders, their councils, their synods and beyond those the ordinary church members.

The South African Government controls a formidable arsenal and legal apparatus of repression. Detention without trial, bannings, house arrest, a network of informers and agents, give the churches no leeway to engage in political activity, which in the South African context, means almost any social or economic action on behalf of the black population, or any pleas for social justice. The law makes it possible to eliminate organizations seen as prejudicial to the state, as was done on 19 October 1977 when the Christian Institute was closed down together with 17 black community groups and their assets seized and sequestrated to the state. In February 1980, Bishop Desmond Tutu, the General Secretary of the SACC, had his passport confiscated, seemingly to prevent him conferring with Christian colleagues and donor agencies outside South Africa.

Faced with a growing campaign against apartheid in North America and Europe which was unstoppable, the nationalists turned again to attack the SACC. In the summer of 1980 P W Botha, the Prime Minister of South Africa, directly accused the SACC in a Republic Day address of channelling money from abroad to foment unrest, and he also accused parts of the mass media of playing a supporting role in the onslaught on South Africa.

In his public reply to Mr Botha, Bishop Desmond Tutu accused him of lying. In his press statement on 30 May 1980 he said-

'I am sick and tired of government officials making allegations such as those of Mr Botha today. If they have the evidence of our nefarious activities why for goodness sake don't they charge the SACC in open court? Our books are, I repeat, open to scrutiny by all and sundry.

'We have used massive funds to provide legal defence for those charged under the often vicious security legislation dreamed up by the nationalists.

'If we say that of those so defended nearly 70 per cent have been acquitted, and of those not so defended up to 85 per cent have been convicted, then we have a record to be proud of.

'We have used these funds to assist with administration of justice because we believe firmly that everyone is entitled to the best defence possible — that is a hallowed canon in free and democratic countries.

'We have provided assistance for the families of banned and detained persons as well as of political prisoners. If doing this makes us guilty of a heinous crime, then, Mr Botha, we plead guilty and will go on doing it despite your fulminations.

'We have used funds for unemployment self-help projects and for community development schemes. If this is helping to foment unrest, then we are standing words on their heads, because we are helping to defuse a volatile and tense situation.

'The prime minister pours scorn on non-violent methods of bringing about change in South Africa. Does he mean us to understand then that the only methods that can bring about change are to be violent ones?

'We are facing a serious situation which is rapidly deteriorating. I urge the prime minister to stop playing politics and looking for scapegoats. Let us all together deal with this problem.

'Mr Botha in his allegations about the SACC, is lying and he knows he is lying. We don't use the kind of methods the nationalists exposed in the info scandal.' Bishop Tutu concluded by challenging Mr Botha and Mr Kruger to a public debate on the aims and methods of the SACC.

But every time the apartheid government takes action against the churches it risks worldwide condemnation and further damage to its image. It is therefore useful to have some apparently independent opposition to what the SACC is saying. Such opposition has been provided by the breakaway and non-representative bodies, the Christian League of Southern Africa, the Catholic Defence League and the Anglican Reform League. Each seeks for an eschatological handhold against the mainstream of thinking and activity in their own churches. They condone apartheid and remain silent before the outrages perpetrated in its name. They also remain silent in the face of white economic privilege. They say what whites in an embattled situation would wish to hear. They defend the policies of the government.

These small organizations are all actively political bodies parading as religious ones. They attempt to destroy church unity and have little to do with propagating the Gospel. They deny to the churches any right to engage in political activity while they themselves are political pressure groups. They discount the value of the vast network of co-operative Christian activity conducted for humane ends which is the main focus of ecumenical bodies such as the SACC and beyond it the WCC.

The full details of how the Christian League became entangled in the Grand Design of Dr Eschel Rhoodie are not yet known, but there is no longer any doubt that it became a front organization for the South African government.

The founder, the Rev Fred Shaw, set up the CLSA in 1974 on his own initiative because he saw the direction taken by the SACC and its affiliated partners overseas to be contrary to the South African way of life as he understood it. The CLSA began to put out a newsletter called *Encounter* which circulated mainly to Protestant clergy in southern Africa. There was a small network of interested people overseas to whom it was also mailed.

To strengthen *Encounter* and boost its circulation inside South Africa was a simple part of the DOI plan. Any intensification of non-governmental campaigns against the SACC and the WCC diverted attention away from the increasing isolation of the NGK, the Dutch Reformed Church, which supported Afrikaner nationalism. The DOI had already helped an existing news magazine *To The Point* which reflected white South African viewpoints on many issues. It provided funds to increase the print run and to expand its circulation to key people and organizations around the world. An enlarged *Encounter* could be made to do the same kind of job for the Christian community as *To The Point* did for the political and business communities. In addition a German language equivalent was started to promote apartheid, South Africa's position, and *Vox Africana* met this need. One of the intermediaries chosen to provide money discreetly to the CLSA was the American businessman John McGoff. When at least one large donation from McGoff to the CLSA became public knowledge during the investigations into the Information scandal, the Rev Fred Shaw explained it as simple Christian charity.

John McGoff is a Michigan newspaper publisher who first visited South Africa in 1968 at the suggestion of Les de Villiers, then an Information Counsellor and later Deputy Secretary of the Department of Information. McGoff became a regular visitor to South Africa and a personal friend of Dr Connie Mulder with whom he became a partner in a game farm in the Transvaal. He became the centre of an informal network of American Midwestern businessmen who supported South Africa, and he himself became engaged in a series of business deals in South Africa. One of his companies printed Afri-Comics for J van Zyl Alberts, who was also managing director of the pro-government *To The Point*. McGoff was involved in an abortive attempt to buy the South African Associated Newspapers Group in 1975 in the interest of the DOI and he became the central figure in the Department of Information's most ambitious project aimed at influencing the thinking of political and business leadership in the United States. This was the attempt to buy the *Washington Star* newspaper which, it was hoped, would neutralize the powerful and critical *Washington Post* and give South Africa its own secret editorial voice in the heart of America. After months of negotiation and the expenditure of hundreds of thousands of dollars, the McGoff bid was foiled and a plan was substituted to buy the *Sacramento Union*, another influential paper, especially with Californian legislators. His partner in this exercise was Richard Mellon Scaife.[5] There were other secret projects to undermine certain politicians and to support others in California into which the purchase fitted.

The urgent need to retain a powerful political and business lobby in the United States arose from South Africa's nightmare of being robbed of oil supplies by internationally-backed sanctions. South Africa is rich in minerals, largely self-sufficient in food and most commodities and has almost unlimited reserves of coal — but no oil. Its war machine and economy depend on imported oil. The long-term chance of survival is SASOL — a process for making fuel oil from coal — but it is costly. One estimate forecast the possibility of SASOL producing a third of South Africa's oil needs by the mid-eighties, and to do this American expertise and capital are essential. McGoff claims to have interested American businessmen and to have mobilized a strong pressure group to get the Export-Import Bank to reverse the limitations imposed on South African investment. An American company, the Los Angeles based FLUOR Engineering and Constructors, won the major contract to build the processing plant for SASOL II and is likely to work on SASOL III. Their contract also includes the possibility of the new process being used in the States.

McGoff was also a friend of President Ford dating from his days in Congress. As he flew back and forth to South Africa on social and business visits he was able to act as courier for Vorster to Ford.[6] Ex-President Ford was subsequently retained to address a large convention of businessmen in Houston, Texas, sponsored by the South African Foreign Trade Organisation, for which he received a fee of $10,000. At the same convention John McGoff made a strongly political speech attacking Senator Clark, a powerful critic of the South African regime.

All of this and a great deal more was unravelled by the official Erasmus Commission in Pretoria in 1979, which showed how $10.5 million was made available to McGoff to buy the American newspaper on behalf of South Africa. This was done via a secret fund through the Swiss front company Thesaurus, with almost entirely ineffective precautions on the conditions of its use or return. (This was apart from interest on an earlier loan obtained by McGoff and the money he received for other projects.) The Commission went on to describe what happened. The entire profits of the newspaper were to be paid to Thesaurus, but in the first years no profit was paid. However, $380,000 were repaid, leaving an outstanding debt of $10,120,000. In 1977 McGoff was involved in a lawsuit in the States which obliged him to reveal his full assets and liabilities. Naturally he was frightened that the huge secret loan might be revealed. McGoff proposed an arrangement with Dr Rhoodie by which he (McGoff) returned $4,970,000 of the loan and the two men agreed that the balance should be written down to $1 million, cancelling off some $4,150,000 of the debt. In March 1978 the remaining debt of $1 million was sold to McGoff's partner, Leipprandt, for $30,000.

McGoff had also been asked to buy a 50 per cent share in UPITN, the global television news service whose headquarters are in London. This was part of another wide-ranging covert international plan to gain control of significant centres of the most influential news media in different parts of the world. Once more little control was exercised over McGoff who bought it 'on behalf of the Republic of South Africa, but acquired it for himself', said the Erasmus Commission.

It is in this context that we need to see the connection between McGoff and the Christian League. Under pressure from the press the Rev Fred Shaw had admitted receiving some $20,000 from McGoff, but says it was to help *Encounter*. He has repeatedly denied that the League received support from the former Department of Information's secret funds.

In October 1978 Shaw told the American newspaper the *Atlanta Journal and Constitution* that he knew nothing about McGoff's attempt to buy the influential *Washington Star*. 'Mr McGoff,' he told the reporter, 'impressed me as a most open, honest Christian and one of the finest men I have ever spoken to.' 'If he does something.' he went on, 'he could not care two hoots if you know it or not. He was a Methodist lay preacher but he was disgusted with the church's involvement in political issues. He said his contribution to the Christian League was what he would normally have given to the church.'

In the wake of the report of the third Erasmus Commission the *International Herald Tribune* carried a story on 20 July 1979 of how McGoff had issued a 1,200 word statement which he printed on the front page of (his own) *Sacramento Union*. In this he denied being an agent or front for any foreign government, but did not deny the findings of the official South African investigating commission that he used $11.5 million from the covert propaganda fund to help him acquire the *Sacramento Union* and a half interest in the UPITN and that this enabled him to bid for the *Washington Star*. McGoff still refused to talk to reporters.

Back in South Africa, following the report of the Methodist committee of enquiry into the CLSA and the decision of the Methodist Conference to repudiate the League, Shaw again commented that the suggestion of aid from government funds was 'utter rubbish'.[7]

In November 1978 when stories were circulating in the South African press that the League had received thousands of rands from the defunct DOI, the President of the Methodist Church in South Africa, Dr D C Veysie, stated that he was not satisfied with the Rev Shaw's explanations regarding the League's funding and challenged him to say why he was not prepared to disclose the full sources of his organization's income. 'I have done this as I believe his remarks and refusal to reveal the sources of his organization's funds reflect on the institution of the ministry of the Methodist Church of Southern Africa as a whole.'

Shaw had said in comment: 'If we received money from the South African Government and it is given us (so) that we do not know who gave it to us and with no strings attached, then the South African Government must be praised as the most Christian Government in the world because it is only helping aid the defence of the faith.'

Echoing his boss's point Graeham Blainey, the CLSA's London representative, wrote to the *Methodist Recorder*, 11 January 1979, to say: 'The CLSA does not receive money with "strings attached". The exact details of the origin of our funds I do not, at this stage, know. Keeping the accounts is not my job.'

Again as reported in the American newspaper the *Atlanta Journal and Constitution*, 13 May 1979, Shaw, in a telephone interview, repeated his earlier denial of ever receiving money from the South African Government.

The South African newspaper *The Star*, 19 September 1979, revealed a chronology of events which had not been pieced together before. In November 1977, the Rev Shaw wrote to his supporters saying that he could not guarantee a salary to staff after 30 November 1977, and that he would have to cancel visits to Britain and the States. Shortly afterwards the American publisher John McGoff offered to pay 'the full account involving *Encounter*'.

'In March 1978 Mr Shaw told a meeting in Pretoria that he had been promised about R300,000 in cash. This was told to *The Star* by a source who has provided other accurate information about the League. The source added that Mr Shaw had been appealing for only R60,000.

'According to the document Dr Rhoodie released to *Elseviers*, R229,314.81 was spent on project "Bernard" (Christian League of South Africa) by March 31st, 1978. The project was numbered G11c.

'In a letter sent to the Minister of Finance, Senator Owen Horwood, early in May 1978, Dr Connie Mulder, former Minister of Information, asked the senator to authorise the expenditure of R320,000 in the year 1978/79 on project G11c.

'The money was to come from the secret fund account of the Information Department. The letter reproduced in a report of the Erasmus Commission was the one on which Senator Horwood cancelled his initials and signature.

'*The Star* also established that the Christian League bought the house it occupies at 702 Church Street, Pretoria, early in April 1978. Mr Shaw, the paper reported, had no comment to make. The purchase price was R38,000.'

Chapter 7 examines in greater depth, the attempted subversion of North America but it is necessary at this point to tell part of the story. In the summer of 1978 the Christian League was planning an ambitious speakers tour of North America. It included a brief visit to Britain on the way there and on the way back. The tour was a full-scale barnstorming exercise in which a network of local sponsors across the States was mobilized to organize a schedule of public meetings, media events, interviews with the press and on the air and talks with businessmen. The theme: *Africa. Its politics and religion . . . can you make a balanced decision*? The advance colour brochures widely distributed in the States by the local organizers went on: 'A team of experts from Africa will be visiting the USA . . . give them a hearing. Book them NOW for a Service or Conference, or arrange a Special Meeting for them at your Church, School, College or Service Club.'

The team consisted of the Chairman Fred Shaw, their Information and Research man the Rev Chin Reddy, a Hindu convert and ex-Minister of the Evangelical Bible Church, the Rev David Kingdon, a member of the Editorial Board of *Encounter* and a Baptist, Father Arthur Lewis and Pastor Musa, billed as a renegade Marxist converted to Christianity, and finally Professor Frank Coleman, a Scottish Catholic migrant who had worked in Rhodesia (now Zimbabwe) and South Africa and was now an economic historian at Rhodes University.

Such a tour is both costly and difficult to organize without the resources of a substantial public relations effort. The tour was planned to last some six weeks and to cover the length and breadth of the States plus Toronto in Canada before returning to London and then home to South Africa.

In the course of this planning there was an exchange of correspondence between Fred Shaw and an American film company with close South African connections. Its managing director was entertained by Mr and Mrs Shaw at their home in Pretoria. This company was to supply the slide programme and the equipment on which to show it during the tour. In a letter from the film company, there are two paragraphs which leave no doubt that the CLSA had dealings with the South African Government and expected funding from it.

The letter begins 'Dear Fred' and congratulates him on his new offices and 'the fine way in which your organization is developing'. Lower down are the two extracts which are significant:

'I hope you have been able to get clearance from the government for the purchase of the projectors, recorder, dissolver and screen. I believe I left you the figures of the approximate cost on these. We should have this bank draft in hand no later than September 1st . . .'

While this might be referring to a request for government clearance to spend money abroad, can the paragraph below be interpreted in the same way?

> 'You will note in our Agreement that the process of preparation for the dual projector presentation is considerably more costly than for the single and that if you were to select the dual presentation there was to be a $500.00 payment beyond the basic $5,000 for which you have applied to the government.'

The dateline for this letter is 9 August 1978. It was the time when the controversy about the CLSA's funding was at its height and only a few weeks before Fred Shaw was denying *any* possible government connection.

The tour was naturally of great importance to the South African information effort. On his return to South Africa in October 1978 Shaw, in an exclusive interview with the government backed newspaper *The Citizen*, 2 November 1978, said that he and his speakers had laid the foundation for tremendous re-investment in South Africa — potentially running to many billions of dollars.

In a series of long interviews given to the editor of *Elseviers* Dr Eschel Rhoodie specified various ways in which Western opinion was manipulated. He stated that the government took charge of the Christian League and transformed and extended it. He told how it was given its own publication *Encounter*. He maintained that the Minister of Defence P W Botha, now Prime Minister, approved the plans and so did John Vorster. The article reproduced sections of a project list and financial statement which showed the CLSA as Project G11-C, code name Bernard. Furthermore he claimed that payments included R10,000 to the Rev Fred Shaw for his defence costs in a pending court case. The total spent on the CLSA had amounted to R229,314.81. In the financial summary, a salary of R13,200 is also listed as a direct government charge.

In the same series of articles Rhoodie revealed that the prestigious white Nederlands Gereformeerde Kerk, the very heart of the Afrikaner religion, had been secretly funded by the Department of Information from 1974 to the tune of some £66,000. Following publication the NGK was forced to admit that this was correct and that the leadership had thought fit to hide the fact from its membership.

On 29 November 1979, in the nationalist newspaper *Die Transvaler*, Pik Botha, the Foreign Minister of South Africa, admitted in a statement that the CLSA had received funds from the defunct Department of Information. The League however maintains its innocence.

As the Muldergate story continues to unfold, the pattern

repeats itself. When a secret project is revealed the parties concerned deny clandestine dealings or connections until cover is irreparably blown.

As recently as 6 March 1980, Graeham Blainey, in the pages of *The Methodist Recorder*, denied any connection between the CLSA and government funding: 'We totally and completely reject the suggestion that we have been in receipt of South African government funds. The fact that individuals would attempt to use this as a smear is a demonstration of their dishonesty.'

On 14 May the 23 volumes of evidence of the official Erasmus Commission were published in South Africa. An extract reported in the *Rand Daily Mail,* of 16 May 1980, suggested the CLSA's connection with the defunct DOI. It came in evidence handed to the Erasmus Commission by Louw Reynders, the BOSS accountant, which showed the League 'as one of our organizations'.

Reynders said that, 'on 9 August 1976 R10,000 was advanced to J G Borman MPC and lawyer at Middelburg Transvaal, for possible legal costs of Mr Shaw. To date there is no statement of expenditure or any other details received. It would appear that there has as yet been no legal action.'

In his reply Dr Rhoodie is quoted as saying: 'The court action by the South African Council of Churches against Shaw and the Christian League was pending. The case has already been on the roll twice, but has not been taken any further. We must protect our own organizations and the R10,000 is a required deposit if we are going to fight the case.'

The formidable apparatus of the DOI continues to influence public opinion across the world under the guise of ISSA — Information Service of South Africa. An old aide of Dr Connie Mulder, Louis le Grange, is the new Minister. Judging from the way editors of the church press have been wooed it is clear that Information Officers from the South African Embassy in Britain are charged with the task of keeping in as close touch as possible with the church media and the churches, including wining and dining any journalists whose opinion might be influenced. They also lose no opportunity of quoting the activities of the Christian League and Catholic Defence League as representative of the feelings of the Christian community in South Africa.

During the last week of January 1980 Fred Shaw, accompanied by two Dutch Reformed Church ministers from Cape

117

Town, the Rev Hannes Ebersohn and Rev K Beukes, visited the
UK, and spoke at a meeting at Caxton Hall on 'The Future of
Rhodesia', sharing the platform with Nicholas Winterton MP
and Sam Swerling of the Monday Club. The two ministers were
trawling for material for something called 'The Churches Media
Project', a library of audio-visual aids for South African con-
sumption, but Fred Shaw had other plans. He had an appointment with the Charity Commissioners to complain about
Christian Aid against which the CLSA was campaigning.
However, the climax of his visit to the UK was to pursue
negotiations for the purchase of the defunct Anglo-Catholic
newspaper *The Christian World*, which was in the hands of a
receiver, owing creditors some £33,000. Negotiations had been
started by the CLSA's London solicitors and Shaw had been
actively seeking funds from colleagues in the States, Canada and
New Zealand for this new religious publication to be put out
under the banner of the International Christian Network.

He had worked out the staffing, choosing the Dutchman Dr
Vermaat as Editor-in-Chief and planned to bring in Dr Mitchell, a
CLSA staff man from South Africa.[8]

All this demonstrated that the CLSA was not in any way
dismayed by the growing evidence of its government ties in
South Africa but was busy opening new doors as others shut in
its face.

Fred Shaw did not manage to purchase *The Christian World*.
The publication was owned by a body named The Christian
Communication Trust, two of whose trustees were the Bishop
of Truro and Geoffrey Evans, ex-Secretary of the Church
Union. The trustees turned down the South African offer.

In a letter from South Africa to his international mailing list at
the beginning of March 1980, Shaw was still able to write, 'I was
privileged to share in the preparatory work for this publication
which, when it is launched later on in the year, will make a
tremendous impact upon the Christian world.' He also talked of
fresh CLSA initiatives in West Germany and Malawi and an
outreach into Mozambique and Zambia — 'getting behind the
lines' he calls it, a plan, if plan it is, which echoes the Vorster
diplomacy of the early 1970s.*

On the Christian Affirmation Campaign bookstall at their
June 1979 Conference a booklet called *Amnesty for Terrorism*
was being sold. This was a production of the South African

---

* The story has evolved since this text was written and is outlined in a postscript after Chapter 9.

Department of Information in 1978, just one of the half million copies of its various publications in some 13 languages which it prints and distributes around the world.

The Rev Theo Kotze, formerly a Director of the banned Christian Institute in South Africa, said in an address to the Royal Institute of International Affairs in November 1978:

'The disclosures of the last few days and those of previous months expose the desperation of the South African Government in its attempt to deceive the outside world. The simple fact is that the South African system cannot stand the test of truth . . .'

References

1. See the *Observer*, UK, 21 January 1979, and *The Star*, Johannesburg, 9 June 1979.

2. The *Guardian*, 24 January 1980; 25 January 1980.

3. The story also linked the gun, a .32 revolver which was used in the Smit killing, with bullets recovered from the attempted murder in Rome, in October 1975, of the Chilean diplomat in exile Bernardo Leighton, a bitter opponent of General Pinochet.

4. South African *Hansard*, 29 April 1979.

5. Richard Mellon Scaife, American oil and banking magnate, heir to the Gulf Oil family income, director of the Mellon National Bank in Pittsburgh, became chairman of Kern House Enterprises in 1973. This was the parent company of Forum World Features, the professional news service based in London, closed in 1975 as it was being exposed as a CIA front.
   Brian Crozier and Iain Hamilton, both executive staff members at Forum moved to the Institute for the Study of Conflict as its Director and Director of Studies respectively. Forum's library moved with them.
   According to a background paper prepared by State Research in 1977, the ISC operates by offering its 'technical expertise' on 'subversion' and on 'communist influence' to official bodies — including the military, the police, other government bodies and business.

6. See the *Sunday Express*, Johannesburg, 2 December 1979.

7. See the *Observer*, UK, 21 January 1979, Anthony Sampson's article 'The General's White Lies'; and *Johannesburg Star*, 9 June 1979.

8. See also Chapter 4 section on ICN for discussion of the planting of Dr John Mitchell in Britain.

6. Tomorrow the World

As a result of the Muldergate investigations there has been far more interest shown in South Africa itself in who did what and to whom. There has been much less interest in following up the hints of hidden subversion and of widescale bribery in other countries. With few exceptions, investigative journalists seem to have shrugged off the whole affair.

In the topsy-turvy worlds of intelligence and propaganda, or dis-information to use one of the current euphemisms, anything goes. We have become so used to the idea of leaders of states condoning 'dirty tricks', of agents breaking the law, of one powerful country interfering subversively in the affairs of another, that we can no longer be surprised. Nevertheless, these things are important and we should all be alert. We have a right to know the full story when we hear that certain politicans in our own countries have been bribed, or that our intelligence services may be sharing information with counterparts in a country whose record on racism and on human rights must be condemned. We have a right to be warned if our domestic organizations at work or in our social life, such as our churches, are being infiltrated by people who are paid to pursue a parti-cular line whether from the political left or right. But what the political left has always done openly, the far right is now attempting under cover. It is of the utmost importance that these attempts should be exposed.

As far as South Africa is concerned, no one can rest until the final tally of secret projects around the world has been com-pleted. The current official line in South Africa seems to be to preserve all those secret projects connected with the defunct Department of Information as long as they remain uncovered by the press or official enquiries, and to use the time gained to make cosmetic changes to disarm investigation. If, as one gathers, the Christian League is partly financed through an industrial company, the Protection of Business Information Act 1978 makes it impossible to check this by any normal enquiry.

South African government officials must hope that public

interest will wane and that any sense of outrage which stemmed from the Muldergate investigations will be dissipated. They must also hope that the current political shift to the right in the industrialized countries throughout the world may create a climate more sympathetic to their minority régime, in view of the importance of investments, trade in rare minerals and the fight against communism in southern Africa.

This chapter is in the form of a short résumé of what has been going on in relation to Christian communities in several countries. Some are little more than glimpses on which others will need to expand. The methods used differ, but the general pattern of the strategy remains very similar. The countries are dealt with alphabetically and not in order of importance.

Canada

When the CLSA organized its North American speakers' tour for the autumn of 1978, four days were allocated to Canada and return flights were scheduled through Toronto. James Cotter of Ontario, the host, set up meetings and media exposure in advance. Creating sympathetic links with businessmen was one of the CLSA's main objectives on this trip.

One of the organizations the visitors from South Africa met in Toronto was the Confederation of Church and Business People (CCBP), a body set up in 1977 by a number of eminent industrialists to combat the attacks of the 'socially aware' churches and related community organizations on the business world. The directors of the CCBP included John Bradfield, a retired top executive of Noranda Mines Ltd, and G T N Woodruffe, a retired official of the Falconbridge Nickel Mines Ltd. Noranda Mines had been under heavy criticism for their investment plans in Chile while Falconbridge Nickel Mines operate mines in Namibia in defiance of UN and World Court decisions calling for the cessation of all trade and investment in Namibia while it continues to be occupied by South Africa. They were worried, in particular, at the criticism of the operations of multinationals in Chile and in South Africa and the primary focus of their anxiety was the Task Force on Church and Corporate Responsibility. This body is supported by the main Canadian church denominations, acting as watchdogs on Canadian companies. They involved themselves in shareholders' annual meetings, asking for withdrawal from those countries where companies, by their presence if not directly, were giving support to tyrannical régimes.

In June 1978 the Confederation and the South Africa Foundation jointly sponsored a luncheon attended by selected businessmen, clergy and press, to meet John Chettle, the Foundation's American representative, to talk about the situation in South Africa. Chettle's address was subsequently widely circulated. The Foundation is sponsored by companies with investments in South Africa, and presents a sanitised version of *apartheid* to boost the country's image overseas.

Also during 1978 Lubor J Zink, a columnist on an extreme right-wing tabloid the *Toronto Sun*, went via South Africa on an all-expenses-paid trip to observe the elections in Namibia. The editor of the *Catholic Register*, Larry Henderson, and Grant Lennie, the manager of the CCBP, were also there as observers. Lennie issued a lengthy and favourable report upon his return as 'Official Observer of December Elections in Southwest Africa/Namibia' which was extensively distributed. In April 1979 he was in Rhodesia to 'observe' the Rhodesian elections and visited one of the 'homelands' in South Africa afterwards. He praised the 'homelands' policy on his return. Both the *Toronto Sun* and the *Catholic Register* reported favourably upon conditions in South Africa and Namibia.

A frequent visitor to South Africa who supports the policies of the minority government there is Kenneth Hilborn, who is on the staff of the history faculty of the University of Western Ontario. He is a frequent letter-writer to the press and a confirmed opponent of Task Force.

An older association 'Friends of Rhodesia Society' led by Sidney Greenhill, a real-estate man and a former Rhodesian, surfaced again as the 'Recognize Rhodesia/Zimbabwe Committee'. They appear to have close links with John Bulloch, owner of a men's tailor shop and President of the Canadian Small Business Association, who frequently places lengthy advertisements in the *Toronto Globe and Mail* calling for an end to 'terrorism' in Rhodesia and who gave the visitors from the Christian League good publicity.

Fred Shaw met John Bulloch during his visit to Canada in 1978. Later, he approached Bulloch for money to help launch the new international church newspaper project. James Cotter, CLSA's Canadian host, was deeply involved in the plans for this new venture. In December 1979, Cotter was looking for ways to mass distribute flyers and the whole exercise revealed CLSA in the act of a cosmetic change, creating an independently funded paper based in Britain to promote its views.

A new organization called C-Far emerged during 1979. C-Far — Citizens for Foreign Aid Reform — questions the effectiveness of the massive expenditure of Canadian taxpayers' money on aid and the choice of countries which receive it. It seeks to confront what it calls 'the well-organized and highly political church lobby' and produces a tabloid *Church Watch* which quotes favourably and at length from Father Arthur Lewis's booklets and articles and generally takes a vigorously pro-apartheid line on Southern Africa.

Three of the four members of the executive of C-Far are also members of Western Guard, known in Canada as a group given to acts of violence against political enemies and advocating a rabid right-wing ideology. Some of the supporters of anti-apartheid groups have in the past been beaten up. It is in essence a white supremacist organization.

The tone of *Church Watch* closely echoes other right-wing journals such as *Spearhead* and *League Review* in Britain.

Holland — a Post Office for South Africa?

There has always been a close relationship between Holland and South Africa. The original Afrikaans settlers brought their Dutch language and their religion from Holland and the many family and business connections remain. In addition, much of the international diamond business passes through Amsterdam.

But while the Nationalist Government has led South Africa into a position of confrontation with its own black community and with much of the rest of the world, Holland has moved within the mainstream of political, social and religious change. The contributions of recent Dutch governments to developing countries is among the largest in the world. While there are pockets of 'traditional' belief, public opinion is firmly behind action for social justice — a tough nut for South African propaganda to crack. Even the mother NGK in Holland opposes the racialism of the Dutch Reformed Churches in South Africa.

In 1979 the Netherlands Council of Churches, which has nine members including the Roman Catholic Church, accepted a resolution which condemned new investments in South Africa and promised to study a plan for boycotting South African products. In April 1979 the Council asked the Dutch Government to take steps for an effective oil embargo against South Africa.

123

In terms of South African expenditure on counter-information Holland comes below the States, West Germany, Britain and France. There is an active Dutch anti-apartheid movement but only a modest pro-apartheid lobby. Holland, however, is a useful and central post office for the rest of Europe. The airline KLM has distributed 40,000 quarterly copies of the CLSA's magazine *Vox Africana* and shipped bulk supplies of their newspaper *Encounter*. Questions about this were asked in the Dutch Parliament in August 1978. Herbert Jussen, the Dutch businessman and former chairman of the South African magazine *To The Point*, financed by the Department of Information, was a board member of KLM's SA subsidiary until he resigned at the time that the Muldergate investigations began. KLM explained that it also organized the international distribution of *To The Point*, but that both this and the CLSA deal were strictly on a commercial basis.

The setting up of the Netherlands-South African Working Committee pre-dates any of the current controversies since it began in 1961. After eight years of work it became ambitious to extend its activities and set up a communication centre for 'objective information' about South Africa for the whole world. The result was the Foundation for the Study of Plural Societies. Its first effort was a quarterly magazine called *Plural Societies* which had an anthropological flavour designed to appeal to academics who, the organizers argued, were coming increasingly under the influence of anti-apartheid material in their professional magazines. It was in fact an attempt to make South Africa's Bantustan policy respectable. In 1975 it produced a huge set of *Case Studies on Human Rights and Fundamental Freedoms* — five volumes in hardback, each of some 500 pages with well-drawn maps. About 4,000 copies were sent free of charge to university departments and libraries all over the world. The estimated cost of some £200,000 was paid by the Foundation and the works were published by Van Den Berg and Versluis, a small firm in Dordrecht specializing in the publication of material for the SA Embassy in the Hague. One of the associate editors of this work was Professor Nic Rhoodie, brother of Dr Eschel and Denys Rhoodie who worked in the DOI. The Third Erasmus Commission report said about Professor Rhoodie: '. . . the Commission finds it reprehensible in principle that brothers in charge of a government department should be instrumental in channelling such a large income to a brother of theirs . . .'

Another of the editors was Mrs Winifred Crum-Ewing, a free-lance British film scriptwriter with a long record of political opposition within the film union ACTT to motions condemning apartheid and to bans on members working in South Africa. She wrote two of the articles in the *Case Studies*. She and an American, Kurt Glaser, edited all the manuscripts for the publishers, for which they were generously paid. In the interviews Dr Eschel Rhoodie gave to the Dutch magazine *Elseviers*, he named the Foundation as an information front.

One of CLSA's contacts in Holland was Dr John Vermaat of Hilversum, listed as the official Dutch representative for the International Christian Network in early press releases but who has since kept a low profile. He attended the World Council of Churches conference in Jamaica in November 1978 together with the Rev David Kingdon. They both carried credentials from right-wing European newspapers; Dr Vermaat as press representative for *Evangelische Omroep* — the Evangelical Broadcasting Company which supports South Africa with its radio and TV programmes — and David Kingdon for the German paper *Idea*. Dr Vermaat was named by the Rev Fred Shaw as editor-elect of the new international Christian newspaper the League was hoping to publish.*

It was in Holland that Dr Eschel Rhoodie chose to tell the world some of the secret propaganda actions which he had initiated while he was Secretary of Information. Amongst these was Project G-11c, the Christian League of Southern Africa.

The Networks Outpost in New Zealand

At the meeting in London in July 1978 of about 40 Christians from different parts of the world, it was agreed to form the International Christian Network, an organization intended to cock a theological snook at the WCC. The Rev Matthew Calder, the vicar of the large Anglican church of St Mark's in Wellington, was present at this meeting. He spoke in his usual vigorous manner and was duly elected to be the Regional Chairman for Oceania on the Executive Committee. Calder was a long-standing enemy of ecumenism in the church and a leading member of the Selwyn Society — a group of Anglicans totally opposed to church union in New Zealand. He was also the founder member and chairman of the New Zealand Israel Association, an outpost of the British Israel movement. In the preparatory documents

---

* Dr Vermaat has since let it be known that he has broken with ICN because he learnt that the new South African chairman Dominee Ebersohn is a longstanding member of the Broederbond, the Afrikaner secret society.

listing possible recruits to the ICN which the Rev Fred Shaw had drafted earlier in the year when working on the project in Pretoria, the Selwyn Society was one of the bricks in the plan.

In a morning broadcast on New Zealand Radio on 17 October 1978, shortly after his return from Britain, Calder spoke enthusiastically about the formation of the Network. He deplored the fact that the WCC was now run by people from the Third World who 'don't represent standard Christian ideas'. He poured scorn on the opponents of racial oppression and those who saw it as contrary to the Gospel. He was convinced, 'that people didn't know they were oppressed until the WCC told them they were'. He maintained that the WCC grants to liberation movements in southern Africa were 'telling the world that we Christians approve of the massacre of innocent women and children'. The real struggle, he said, was not black versus white, but communism versus Christianity.

On the last Sunday in February 1979 more than a hundred parishioners' cars outside the Takapuna Methodist Church had anti-WCC broadsheets placed under their windscreen wipers. Other churches in Auckland had been similarly leafleted.

The broadsheet, similar in every way to the usual CLSA material distributed in Britain, told of an atrocity in Rhodesia attributed to a 'terrorist' and went on to make a direct link between the event and the WCC's humanitarian aid programme to liberation movements. The message ended: 'Why donate to the WCC? Don't kill a Christian today!'

The New Zealand League of Rights was forced to withdraw the terrorism broadsheet and to make a public apology for misquoting Dr Eugene Blake after action by the Rev Les Clements of the Takapuna Church, but the League continues to be active, distributing slanderous booklets about the ecumenical movement. The League through its international contacts has links with the World Anti-Communist League, with the Christian Affirmation Campaign, with the Christian League of Southern Africa and the International Christian Network through the Rev Calder.

In July 1979 Calder attempted to get support for the ICN in the Wellington Anglican Diocesan Synod. He had no success. In August 1979 Calder was an official guest of the South African Government and invited to visit Namibia. He found time to visit Father Lewis in Rhodesia and was hosted there by the Rhodesian Government at the request of the New Zealand/ Rhodesia Society. In Rhodesia Calder was interviewed on government TV and did radio tapes for Australian and New

Zealand news services. In South Africa he conferred with Fred Shaw about plans to take over a weekly Christian newspaper in Britain (since discovered to be the defunct *Christian World*).[1]

Back in New Zealand Calder was interviewed on the national radio link about his experiences. In his opinion Bishop Muzorewa, Ian Smith and other ministers are 'practising Christians. They are delightful chaps, they are men of vision and of quiet strength and dignity . . . yet the United Nations wants to put the Christians out and the communist guerrillas in . . .' He also said: 'In Namibia the World Council of Churches' money helps SWAPO to kidnap and assassinate. Do-gooders from far off should stay out and let the South Africans bring independence their way.'

West Germany

In the 1950s West Germany was preoccupied with rebuilding its shattered economy. The 'economic miracle' ensured that by the 1960s West Germany was looking for trading partners on a large scale, to exchange raw materials for finished products, and also for investment outlets. By the early 1970s, it was one of the 'big three' involved in trade with[2] and investment in[3] South Africa, alongside the UK and the USA.

It is therefore hardly surprising that the propaganda efforts of South Africa in West Germany have increased and are similar to such efforts in the United Kingdom particularly as applied to the church. West Germany is a fertile breeding ground for anti-communist sentiments and the church is no exception. There is a conservative sub-culture in the church which takes a number of forms. Some of the most prevalent are:

- ☐ opposition to 'modern' theology,
- ☐ rejection of the 'politicization' of the church,
- ☐ German nationalism, which still regards Germany as a whole violently divided by the communists, who are seen as holding one-third of the German nation hostage,
- ☐ anti-ecumenicalism, in particular hostility towards the WCC.

Not all of the groups which could be considered as part of this conservative grouping hold all of these views — many are evangelical groups which would claim to have no political position. Others have taken a clear political position.

127

Mainstream Political Positions

In broad terms, there are two mainstream political views in relation to South Africa within the major West German political parties. The CDU (Christian Democratic Union) takes a position similar to that of the Conservative Party in the United Kingdom ranging in the stance of its members from more or less open support for apartheid to mild criticism. Within the SPD (Social Democratic Party), there is a range of views very much like those within the British Labour Party, ranging from verbal condemnation to the suggestion of various non-violent economic measures against apartheid. The dominant policy has been to separate trade and politics — to make verbal condemnations, but to allow trade and investment to increase.[4] An active minority of MPs ask critical questions (eg about the 'starvation wages' revealed in 1973).[5]

Economic Relations

Many major West German companies invest in South Africa and have subsidiaries there. Some are heavily dependent upon government contracts. Siemens is one example.[6] The involvement of West German firms certainly extends to industries of military significance, such as the electronics industry.

In 1975, the 'nuclear conspiracy' was uncovered. Firms owned or partly owned by the government, which were engaged in nuclear research in West Germany, had provided the technological know-how for the South Africans to produce enriched uranium — the prerequisite for making an atomic bomb (cf ANC, *The Nuclear Conspiracy*; Z Cervenka, B Rogers, *The Nuclear Axis*, (Julian Friedmann, London, 1978).

The major West German banks also play a vital role in supporting the South African economy.[7]

Mainstream Church Positions

The mainstream church positions, particularly within the Protestant church federation (EKD) is verbally critical, but lacking any strong measures to support this criticism of apartheid. There has been strong resistance to the alleged support of the PCR for 'violence' and the WCC's call for an end to investment in South Africa in 1972 has not been taken up. Instead, the EKD has had a series of confidential talks with firms which have produced no tangible results.[8] However, the EKD provided substantial funding for the Christian Institute of South Africa until the Institute was banned in 1977, and it still supports the South African Council of Churches financially and regards it as the body to which it relates ecumenically. The most intense debate about South Africa[9] has taken place within the EKD and it has adopted a position capable of developing into outright opposition to apartheid. This has alarmed those groups in West Germany with interests in South Africa and/or sympathy towards its policies. It has also attracted the attention of the South African propaganda industry.

Conservative Christian Groups

Some of the characteristics of the various conservative Christian groups in West Germany have been detailed above. They are a significant factor and it would be unwise to underestimate their significance in forming church opinion. Whilst their more outlandish postures and policies have little or no effect on the church leadership, they do help to create a situation where what seems to be a 'middle position' is, in fact, quite conservative. It is fairly common for highly influential church leaders in West Germany to reject the 'interference of the church in politics'. Lutheran leaders such as Dietzfelbinger, a former EKD Council Chairman and Wolber, another important Lutheran bishop, used this position, based on a version of Luther's social ethics, to attack the Programme to Combat Racism and the World Council of Churches. This had had a considerable influence on the conservative fringe.

Since the end of the Second World War, there have been a number of political issues on which West German Christians have been deeply divided. One of them was the re-armament of Germany. In the late 1960s the rallying point for conservatives was the 'Eastern Memorandum', a church document which served as a precursor of Willy Brandt's Ostpolitik — the policy of détente towards Eastern Europe, based upon recognition of post-war boundaries. To German nationalists within the church and outside, this seemed to be nothing less than a betrayal. Many of those who left the German Democratic Republic sought an organizational base from which to propagate their form of nationalistic religious conservatism. It was from this sort of clientèle that the Evangelische Notgemeinschaft in Deutschland (Protestant Emergency Fellowship in Germany) was formed. (It was initially called the Notgemeinschaft Evangelischer Deutscher.) After the failure of this campaign against the Eastern Memorandum, the Programme to Combat Racism was the next target for right-wing consternation in the churches.[10]

One of those at the centre of the anti-ecumenical campaign was Professor Peter Beyerhaus of Tübingen University who was also one of the organizers of the First European Confessing Congress in Berlin in May 1974. This was an attempt to set up a rival organization to the World Council of Churches and it ended with a Declaration on Ecumenism which by implication condemned the WCC. It failed largely because evangelicals from the Third World showed little interest in the Western debate about whether individual salvation or justice was the centre of the gospel — for them, both belonged to the Christian witness. The Programme to Combat Racism was one of the targets for Beyerhaus and his colleagues.[11]

The church situation in Berlin at the time of the congress was very tense. A major campaign in *Bildzeitung*, the popular daily paper of Axel Springer, the right-wing newspaper magnate, was being waged against Bishop Scharf, the bishop of West Berlin. The campaign tried to discredit Scharf as a terrorist sympathiser for following his normal practice of prison visiting (which he had carried out under Hitler, and in West and East Germany after the war) and visiting Ulrike Meinhof of the Baader-Meinhof gang.[12]

The attempt of the congress to set itself up as a corresponding theological event to Barmen 1934, the beginning of the organized church struggle against Hitler, was completely rejected by Scharf.

The Notgemeinschaft set up a counter-programme to the PCR to collect for the 'victims of terrorism' in southern Africa and collected at least DM20,000. There was also an 'Emergency Fellowship' in Namibia engaged in right-wing political and church activity.

In addition, members of the Evangelical Alliance were provided with travel grants to visit South Africa as were a group of students from the church seminary in West Berlin under Professor Jürgen Winterhager. On his return, Winterhager gave an interview to the Evangelical Alliance in which he said that he had not noticed any systematic discrimination during his stay in South Africa. Papers published by the West German Protestant Press Service (EPD) showed that Winterhager and his students received financial support from the South African DOI.[13]

Propaganda

The South African Government obviously regards the West German churches as a key area in the propaganda war. A hostile West German church exerting pressure for sanctions and boycotts could severely undermine the strong co-operation between West Germany and South Africa.

The main German publication produced by the Department of Information is the Journal *Südafrika* which is distributed to public figures such as MPs and journalists and particularly to ministers in the Protestant churches. The World Council of Churches has been a particular target of the Embassy. A series of advertisements under the heading 'Churches without a mandate' followed the WCC's decision in August 1974 to extend the Programme to Combat Racism. South Africa's official response, according to Dr Eschel Rhoodie, was to make available a budget of around £600,000 annually for propaganda purposes in West Germany. This included subsidizing the occasional advertisements in national papers by the Club of Ten[14] and the special printing and delivery to Holland of a German language quarterly *Vox Africana* published by the Christian League in Cape Town and mailed to some 40,000 Protestant clergymen, 99 per cent of whom lived in West Germany, by means of the KLM distribution department at Schipol Airport in Amsterdam. It also included a sum of some £53,000 a year as a grant to a religious group within the Protestant churches in Germany whose task was to oppose the anti-apartheid campaigns developing in the churches.

This organization has now been identified as the Evangelische Notgemeinschaft in Deutschland or END for short. The launching of END was announced in the press in December 1973 when its objectives were briefly described as working to stop church contributions to terrorists in southern Africa.

In July 1974 members of END's executive, Dr R Sauerzapf and Pastor J Ruff, travelled at South Africa's expense to Windhoek, Johannesburg and Pretoria where they established a small committee of clergymen who were to be responsible for the distribution of relief funds from END. The TV ZDF news magazine and the newsletter of the German-South African Working Group gave them publicity. In November 1974,

8,000 copies of END's journal *Erneurung und Abwehr* or *E and A* for short, were sent to all parishes. The contents were propaganda for apartheid South Africa.

In August and September 1974 Dr Peter Beyerhaus visited South Africa where he met Dr Vorster, Fred Shaw and Father Arthur Lewis. Professor Sauerzapf wrote in the December issue of *E and A* that the series of lectures given by Dr Beyerhaus on his visit had proved very useful to Father Lewis.

In October 1975, END brought out a special double issue of *E and A* which was undiluted pro-apartheid propaganda.

In September 1978 an alliance of organizations which consisted of old fascist and neo-fascist groups, traditional Christian groups, and groups working on behalf of trade and cultural links with the white minority in South Africa linked up with END.

In the planning document written in the Pretoria office of the CLSA in May 1978, which prepared the ground for the forthcoming foundation of the International Christian Network, Dr Sauerzapf is listed next to Dr Peter Beyerhaus as the main West German contact. With the help of Dr Beyerhaus, the END and the CLSA were able to get a foothold inside the mainly theological and traditionalist group called the Fellowship of Confessing Christians. It was the CLSA's intention to work within this umbrella organization to undermine the WCC (see Chapter 4).

References

1. Exchange of correspondence and report of Rev Calder to ICN, 1979-80.

2. R First *et al, The South African Connection*, p 137.

3. R Rode, *Die Südafrikapolitik*, p 367.

4. *ibid* Chapter 3, pp 30-131, esp 129-31.

5. *ibid* pp 105-8.

6. *ibid* pp 168-71.

7. *ibid* pp 196-8, cf WCC, *The World Council of Churches and Bank Loans to Apartheid.*

8. R J Williamson, *Alternative Strategies?*

9. R Rode, op cit p 120.

10. K Ahlheim, K Wiesinger, *Auf einem Auge blind.*

11. W Kunneth, P Beyerhaus, *Reich Gottes oder Weltgemeinshaft?* also Ch 5.

12. H Albertz *et al*, *Pfarrer, die dem Gewalt dienen?*

13. *Epd Documentation* 45a/75, 22.10.1975.

14. Two of the important propaganda arms of South Africa in the 70s were the so-called Club of Ten and the South African Foundation. The Club of Ten sponsored large, expensive pro-South African advertisements in prestigious British, Dutch and West German newspapers. The Ten were a small group of wealthy South African businessmen who worked hard to protect their anonymity. Its London consultant for a long time was Gerald Sparrow, a former judge in the International Court of Bangkok, and it was he who commissioned the adverts. In the *Sunday Times*, 25 June 1978 he revealed that he had been chosen to front a campaign 'to deceive the western press' and promote the cause of apartheid and that the whole operation was funded and controlled by the South African Department of Information. Sparrow said that his go-between in London was the former Director of Information at South Africa House.

On 23 February 1977 the Club of Ten ran a quarter page advert in the *Guardian* with photos of seven Jesuits and nuns murdered in Rhodesia, asking, 'who was responsible?' and accusing the World Council of Churches. Similar adverts appeared in West Germany. The Club's attack on the WCC was part of a concerted campaign which also included the CLSA.

The South Africa Foundation was established in 1959 and claimed to be an independent organization financed by private enterprise. Throughout Western Europe it strives for good relationships with pro-South African organizations and claims to distribute unbiased information and research at a high level. One cf its most important themes is that of maintaining investor confidence in South Africa. It commands substantial financing and has offices in Paris, London, Bonn and Washington. Its publications, given away free to government officials, universities and businesses include the annual *Intelligence Digest*, the quarterly *South Africa International* and the monthly *South Africa Foundation News.*

In the UK it co-operates with UKSATA, the body promoting trade links with South Africa. In West Germany it has strong ties with the Deutsche-Südafrikanische Gesellschaft (DSAG) headed by Dr R Gruber, the Foundation's director in Bonn. The DSAG also receives financial subsidies from the Foundation.

Similar groups exist in Holland, Switzerland, France and the USA. In the USA the most important work has been personal contacts, sponsored trips by key decision-makers to South Africa and links in the diplomatic missions, especially relationships with mineral industries and the IMF. See *New African*, May 1978.

7. Alliances in the United States

The real importance of South Africa to the United States is almost negligible in relation to US concerns world-wide. The Republic has only one per cent of all US overseas investment, and is of little interest as a trading partner since most of its exports are concentrated on Western Europe. It offers no oil, and as an import market is of rather small and static size — owing to the poverty of the great majority of its people. In military terms, it is far from the major flash-points of primary concern to US defence planners, which are mainly in Latin America and various parts of Asia and Europe. Nevertheless, the United States is clearly the primary target for South Africa's propaganda machine, both direct and indirect. The objective: to convince Americans and their government that South Africa is of vital strategic and economic importance in the fight against communism.

Although South Africa is small in relation to the rest of the world as an investment area, most of the real giants of American business operate there: General Motors, IBM, the oil companies. In relation to the rest of sub-Saharan Africa, the Republic seems important, with R1,492m in US investment as compared to R4,504m in Africa as a whole in 1978.[1] 539 American companies maintain links with South Africa in terms of direct corporate investment and bank loans, including some of the biggest American banks.[2] Trade, while unimpressive, is increasing steadily and South Africa's imports from the United States showed that the most important category was of various strategic hardware, including aircraft, machinery of all kinds, telecommunications equipment and computers.[3]

Added to the investment of some of the American economic giants in South Africa, which lobby on its behalf in Washington and through the propaganda organization the South Africa Foundation, there is a growing military interest. When the Suez Canal was closed, the South Africans hammered the theme of the 'Cape route' being of strategic importance to the oil routes from the Gulf to the Western countries. This theme has been taken up, first by a few retired World War II veterans and then by right-wing 'strategic planners'. Although an extremely weak argument which is in any case made irrelevant by the functioning of the Canal, there are now many high officials in the Pentagon who appear to accept it and especially the related argument about the Soviet 'menace' to the Indian Ocean. With very good contacts in the military and intelligence establishments, South Africa has capitalized on the 'communist threat' to extract military and technological support from Washington, often with one government department acting without the knowledge or approval of another. In particular, the Defence and Commerce Departments frequently arrange military deliveries to South Africa without consultation with the State Department.[4]

Intelligence co-operation has also been an area of spectacular growth, the more right-wing officials of the CIA obviously taking a leading role. Joint operations, unauthorized by the Administration or Congress, to promote the South African invasion of Angola in 1975 have become public knowledge, thanks to the exposure by the Angolan task-force leader John Stockwell.[5]

Running through these various connections, however, and of major importance in its own right, is the close affinity between the extreme right-wing in the United States and the white minority in South Africa, purely on racist grounds. It is becoming increasingly obvious that the hard-line white supremacists of the American South, far from fading away as a result of civil rights legislation, are in fact finding support and inspiration from the apartheid policies of South Africa. Fanatical and violent organisations such as the Ku Klux Klan and groups like the John Birch Society, which are often allied with fundamentalist religious groups appear obsessed by the subject of race. Such groups become doubly dangerous with the provision of millions of dollars from sympathetic millionaire backers who also offer their newspapers and radio to the cause, and are providing fertile ground for South African propaganda and subversion across the United States with a particular concentration in the Deep South.

No wonder, then, that even the South Africans can hardly believe their luck — and the only fly in the ointment is the reputation for racial fanaticism of their most enthusiastic supporters. In his report on a 'contact tour' of several Southern states in 1975, A J van der Wal of the South African Information

Service in New York reported an appearance on a religious radio programme, and contact with at least one former missionary. He concluded:

> 'In spending the weekend with Mr [Jim] Jacobson [a former visitor to South Africa sponsored by the Department of Information] it became very clear that our image is most definitely improving in America. There is no doubt about the fact that the middle of the road American is leaning towards us. I also believe that at this stage we should start thinking about a weeding out process amongst contacts in the South, because some of our friends are so far to the "right" that it definitely hurts our image in associating with them.'

Speaking of 'one of our staunchest supporters in the South', who provided access to the media throughout the southern States and an introduction to most 'opinion formers' in the area, van der Wal added regretfully, 'unfortunately for us however he is very closely linked with the extreme "Citizens Council"[6] of Jackson (Mississippi).'

A Challenge from the Churches

The main threat to South Africa's growing alliance with the right-wingers of America seemed to be coming, in the mid-1970s, from the major Protestant denominations and in particular their National Council of Churches (NCC) based in New York. It had created a special office, the Interfaith Center for Corporate Responsibility (ICCR), to spearhead shareholder actions against corporate investment in South Africa, and had also shown considerable muscle in its opposition to American banks lending to the Republic.

The ICCR, after several years of research, appeals to the churches and direct action at shareholder meetings, now involves 10 major Protestant churches, 40 Catholic orders and some other religious groups. The bank campaigns too have grown from small beginnings to achieve some major victories. In April 1979, for example, the city of Berkeley in California passed the Berkeley Responsible Investment Ordinance, the first time that a city was directed to withdraw its funds from any banks lending to South Africa. Many major churches as well as other institutions have withdrawn their very considerable accounts from the banks concerned; they have done the same in relation to a few of the companies doing business in South Africa. The issue has been a major one on college campuses, and several universities decided, as a result, to withdraw their financial support from banks and companies with an investment in South Africa.

In April 1980 the South Africa Foundation, which had been investigating the disinvestment campaign in the United States, concluded that the danger it posed to the régime in South Africa was substantial.[7] It pointed out that there were more than 2,000 local, state, regional and national organizations across the country committed to some action in this area. It estimated that these groups had a total financial power — operating funds, institutional support and personal donations — estimated at nearly R87,000 million. There was evidence, the report said, that trade unions were being drawn in and if they decided to withdraw their pension funds from those institutions which were shareholders in South African companies, the economic shock-wave for South Africa would be profound.

South Africa's Answer

One of the most important and daring ventures undertaken by South Africa's Department of Information, in conjunction with BOSS, was the campaign to seize control of certain news media, including newspapers, radio and TV stations throughout the United States. To achieve this, an alliance was set up with sympathetic right-wingers who were already involved, in a small way, in the news business as proprietors. Recent investigative journalism has built on the Erasmus Commission's work and revealed considerable detail about the use of Michigan publisher John McGoff and Indiana publisher Beurt SerVaas as channels for South African takeovers of important media. McGoff almost succeeded in taking over the *Washington Star*, the only rival to the *Washington Post* in the nation's capital.[8] He admitted early in the DOI investigation that he had given money to CLSA (see Chapter 5) and that this was what he would normally have given to the church. SerVaas, who owns the reconstituted *Saturday Evening Post*, has consistently used it as an organ for South African propaganda, some of it actually paid advertisements which were presented as objective reports.[9]

The operations of the DOI in the United States are now known to have covered a wide range, including not only the takeover of news media but also interference in political campaigns, intense lobbying of members of Congress and the administration in Washington, advertising campaigns, and a general strengthening of contacts with their supporters, including those extreme right-wingers whom even van der Wal found a little embarrassing. What has not so far been investigated is the extension of this campaign into the heart of the greatest threat to US support for South Africa, as seen from Pretoria: the churches.

In the long interview with the Dutch magazine *Elseviers*, Dr Eschel Rhoodie has described how the DOI planned to oppose the South African Council of Churches and its international supporters, especially the World Council of Churches: 'To be able to oppose this influence, the government took over the Christian League of South Africa which was expanded and reorganized with its own influential newspaper *Encounter*.'

According to the budget costings which he also released to the magazine, Defence Minister P W Botha (now Prime Minister of South Africa) had approved the plan and even authorized the payment of its organizer, the Methodist minister Fred Shaw, from State funds.

Documents released by Dr Rhoodie show details of Project G Number G-11c, code-named Bernard. The documents reveal the aim of this Project G to be intervention in church affairs inside South Africa and also in other countries, particularly the United States. The methods proposed were the use of personal contacts, conferences, news bulletins, regular publications and other activities.

Church Mercenaries

In extreme right-wing circles in the United States there is often a strange fascination with both religious justifications of political opinions, and imposition of those opinions by means of extreme violence. This often takes the form either of attacks on black people locally, or of mercenary service with armies anywhere that seem to be fighting people of other races — albeit in the name of opposing communism. It is striking that many of the most active supporters of South Africa within the churches have a military background, and that their most useful allies are some members of the powerful American Legion, which represents the veterans of many American wars including those in Korea and Vietnam. Veterans are the major source of recruits to the mercenary armies of southern Africa. Several mercenary recruitment organizations call themselves 'Christian'.

In the June 1980 edition of the mercenary journal *Soldier of Fortune*, amongst the classified advertisements for all kinds of weaponry, books on garrotting and knuckleduster paper-weights, the following appeared:

> 'Wanted. Patriots, especially military veterans, who are interested in preparing for the soon-coming political, social, economic and military disruption of our country. Write Christian Patriots Defense League or Citizens Emergency Defense System, Box 565K, Flora, 111.'

The author was not surprised to receive a copy of a letter written to CLSA's Fred Shaw from one of these mercenary groups. Dated 8 August 1978, it is from the International Security Force, 249 Church Street, Elberton, Georgia, and reads as follows:

> 'I have recently received a copy of your newspaper *Encounter* and would like to offer the services of my organization in the conflict between the Christian community and communism on the African continent. We are a group of Vietnam combat veterans who feel that the differences between Christianity and communism must finally be settled on the battlefield. The slaughter of innocent whites and blacks in Rhodesia is indicative of the teachings of communism.'

Hundreds, if not thousands of these American veterans signed up as mercenaries in the Rhodesian civil war, and before that in Angola and elsewhere. Their actions showed only too clearly that their idea of 'Christianity' is killing and maiming black people. Some of those who remain in the United States support the cause by racist and pro-South African propaganda.

CLSA Recruits Bob Slimp

The Reverend Colonel Robert L Slimp is a retired army chaplain who now lives in Columbia, South Carolina. He has seen service in many theatres of war. Back in Georgia in 1972 he became Lieutenant Colonel aide-de-camp to Governor George Wallace of Alabama who espoused traditional Christian values but was better known for his emotional racism and hatred of left-wingers and liberals. Bob Slimp and George Wallace were fiddle and bow. Slimp, the combat veteran and clergyman with a degree in journalism and a passionate view about the Red Menace to 'Western Christian civilization' was a useful man to have around if you were a politician using fear — fear of subversion, fear of blacks, fear of Reds — to gain votes.

In 1973 the Reverend Colonel retired to help set up and serve as pastor to the Columbia Independent Methodist Church.

He subsequently moved to a Presbyterian church in the same town, and became actively engaged in work with the local post of the American Legion. He made his first visit to South Africa and Rhodesia in 1975, helping to pay for it with articles in the *Borger News Herald*, a Texas daily. These pieces, strongly supportive of official South African policy and of Ian Smith's independent struggle against 'barbaric' liberation movements and world-wide diplomatic treachery, were reprinted by the arch-conservative *Manchester Union Leader* of New Hampshire. No doubt cuttings found their way to Fred Shaw at the CLSA office in Pretoria for it was a short time later that Shaw contacted Slimp.[10] In 1977 Slimp went to South Africa at the invitation of Fred Shaw to address the CLSA's annual meeting in Pretoria, and to visit other places of interest. His ticket and expenses were paid by CLSA.[11] Another guest at that meeting was Dr Peter Beyerhaus.

Either then or shortly afterwards Slimp agreed to act in the United States on behalf of the Christian League and began a programme of speaking engagements, radio interviews, placing articles and preaching. Thus began a period of great activity by the Christian League in North America. *Encounter* was beefed up and free copies mailed to a vastly expanded list of pastors and political leaders in the States.

In December 1977 Fred Shaw visited North America in the company of Dr Raymond Oliver. They stayed as guests of Bob Slimp, made various public appearances and prepared the ground for a major speaker tour for the autumn of 1978. This was to be a key event in the League's campaign to make new friends for South Africa in the States; no amateurish and improvised excursion by a single spokesman, but a meticulously planned and well prepared operation with printed publicity, a network of agents and other contacts to soften up the media ahead of time, book halls and collect audiences for the group of 'experts', representing, at least on paper, a cross-section of religious opinion to lend credence to the League's boast that it represented a broad range of views. The tour was to stick to a tightly packed itinerary taking in 16 major centres around the States. Canada and Britain were included on the outward and return journey.

An active legionnaire was the Reverend Colonel John Hinkel, another retired army chaplain and a public relations consultant with an office in Washington. He agreed to act as a CLSA sponsor and because he was paid a fee, to help set up some

Washington meetings. He registered with the Justice Department as the agent of a foreign national.

Fred Shaw's American Sponsors

There were ten sponsors listed on the League's publicity material. Some are misted in obscurity but others can be recognized. Two have already been identified above.

Major Edgar Bundy, the CLSA sponsor in the state of Illinois, directed The Church League of America. Founded in 1937 as the National Layman's Council by three anti-New Deal Chicago businessmen, it kept files on anyone suspected of leftist tendencies. The information was available, at a fee, to potential employers, organizations screening for credit or political reliability etc. In brief, its task was seen as countering subversion from the left. Today its own literature states its purpose as 'to rekindle the spirit of valiant Christian-Americanism and to counter the strength of Marxian socialism'.

Edgar Bundy is the author of *Apostles of Deceit*, a 544-page exposé 'concerning the creeping epidemic of unbelief and infiltration of communistic propaganda in American churches'. The title was chosen to rebut an earlier and influential book by Ralph Roy called *The Apostles of Discord*[12] which dealt with right-wing groups including those within the churches. Bundy is a prolific writer and other works such as *How the Communists Use Religion*, 162 pages, and *Collectivism in the Churches*,[13] 354 pages, are monuments to his concern. Almost all his writing dwells on common themes such as the evil done by the National Council of Churches[14] and attacks on the World Council for delivering western civilisation 'into the hands of the enemy'. Major Bundy used to organize, and probably still does, 'Counter-Subversive Seminars' which last from two to four days. Each seminar has as its foundation stone *A Manual for Survival*, a Bundy workbook which lists communist techniques of infiltration and subversion; it demonstrates how each person can challenge them. It tells the reader how to support organizations combating subversion, mail counter-subversive literature, expose 'leftist' letters in the press, and book known anti-communists as speakers at local clubs and luncheons.

Major Bundy is a former intelligence officer with the Flying Corps who later became a Baptist minister. He too has been active in the American Legion sponsoring Legion motions against foreign aid, the UN and other targets. He took over

141

control of the Church League of America in 1956 and has expanded it into the largest right-wing 'research' facility of its kind with millions of cross-indexed reference files on 'Communists and fellow-travellers'. It publishes booklets, news bulletins and a substantial catalogue of literature. The Church League is the American publisher of Bernard Smith's *The Fraudulent Gospel* (see Chapter 2).

Bundy is also a close friend and has professional links with Dr Carl McIntyre, the veteran founder of the 'American Council of Churches', a title which resembles that of the National Council of Churches and thus tended to confuse church members. McIntyre, now in his early 80s, continues as active as ever, with his own radio shows and writings. In 1948 he launched the International Council of Christian Churches (ICCC) to harass the World Council of Churches which he saw as a front of Protestant 'apostasy'. He got little support. He organized his own Independent Presbyterian Church after being expelled from the Presbyterian General Assembly. He was deported from Kenya in 1975 after making politically inflammatory remarks about Ian Smith's régime 'upholding civilization'. He was then in the middle of a campaign to disrupt the Nairobi Assembly of the WCC being held later that year.

Charles Keysor of Wilmore, Kentucky, was another sponsor. Keysor, a former PR man who was converted by Billy Graham in Singapore, is now a Methodist minister who teaches journalism at Astbury College. Shaw's introduction to Keysor came from his contact with Howard Ball.

During his 1977 visit Fred Shaw visited Howard Ball in California. Ball was the organizer of the Campus Crusade for Christ which is a very wealthy and aggressive branch of the far right with a programme to 'turn America back to God' together with a political agenda of electing to public office 'real Christians' with a doctrinaire conservative vision. One of the main figures in the Crusade was a charismatic preacher called Bill Bright. In 1977 he was engaged in a billion-dollar money-raising effort to conduct a world-wide evangelistic campaign. With the help of evangelistic businessmen, the first 100 million US dollars had been raised by mid-1979.[15]

The political agenda of the Campus Crusade linked up with a growing political action group called the Christian Voice with headquarters in Pasadena, California. In 1979 it launched its first major national campaign to lift US economic sanctions against Rhodesia, with an 'atrocity' leaflet very similar to those of the CLSA. Although Christian Voice was not a lobbying organization in Washington, it had employed Gary Jarmin, an American Conservative Union lobbyist, as a consultant on a part-time basis. He had begun his political career in anti-communist organizations funded by the Rev Myung Moon's Unification Church. Jarmin said the group was aimed at representing the views of conservative evangelical Christians before Congress, and he is quoted as saying: 'This group is the sleeping giant of American politics. You don't have to organize them. They are already organized better than Republicans and Democrats put together, and they are a vast community with vast resources.' Republican senators Orrin Hatch of Utah, James Maclure of Idaho, Roger Jepsen of Iowa and Gordon Humphrey of New Hampshire are on its advisory board, as are 11 House of Representatives members including Larry McDonald of Georgia, a member of the notorious John Birch Society.[16]

The Campus Crusade provided powerful momentum for the humble Fred Shaw. Among its supporters are TV cowboy Roy Rogers and the Texas oilman and millionaire Nelson Bunker Hunt, a Council member of the John Birch Society. Shaw was undoubtedly fascinated by the ways in which American right-wing church groups raised money, and by the grand style which they were able to adopt — chartered jets between meetings, for instance.

Howard Ball, the Crusade's organizer, was also editor of *Good News* and this was also the name of a conservative movement within the Methodist church which was becoming increasingly significant politically. Ball sent Fred Shaw across America to see Keysor, who was active in this movement. Keysor was a bitter opponent of the WCC and *Good News* was campaigning against it amongst Methodists. The movement accused the church of losing touch with the fundamental beliefs of Christianity and going 'soft' on issues such as homosexuality and 'terrorists in southern Africa'.

Another CLSA sponsor was Joseph Ellenwood of Massachusetts. He too was an active member of the American Legion and the Chairman of its Foreign Relations Commission. Ellenwood was part of a delegation which went to South Africa at the invitation of Donald de Keiffer, South Africa's principal lobbyist in Washington. This Legion visit was paid for by the South African Freedom Foundation, which has since been shown to have been one of the DOI's front organizations.

The American Legion delegation to South Africa got the appropriate VIP treatment from government officials and influential businessmen. As a result the Legion agreed to lobby the American Government to step up investment in South Africa, to hold joint naval manoeuvres once again, to recognize the Transkei bantustan and to carry a series of pro-South African articles in the *Legionnaire*. They also promised to carry out extensive lobbying at grass-roots and national level.

Ellenwood continued his interest in southern Africa, visiting Rhodesia as an observer of the May 1979 elections, this time for the American Tool and Stainless Steel Industry Commission. In relation to the CLSA, Ellenwood told Jeff Nesmith, the *Atlanta Constitution*'s Diplomatic Correspondent, that although he agreed with Shaw to allow his name to be used as a CLSA sponsor, he made no arrangements for them.

Nathaniel Connors Smith of Snyder, Texas, told Jeff Nesmith that he met Shaw when he visited South Africa at his own expense and interest in 1976. Smith is now registered with the Justice Department as the agent of a foreign principal. He is a carpenter and part-time college economics instructor, as well as a pastor in the Calvary Presbyterians, a breakaway southern group. Smith was active in the arrangements for the CLSA speakers' tour and he distributes their literature.

Pat Wood and David McAlvany are partners in a Birchite newsletter called *Citizens Concerned about South Africa* in Colorado. Wood is an investment counsellor. McAlvany is Vice-President of International Investors Inc, a mutual fund with holdings of some 40 million US dollars invested in South African gold mines. The newsletter offers special tours to South Africa. Wood told the Atlanta Constitution on May 13th 1979 that he had nothing to do with the CLSA.

The Case of the Rev Lester Kinsolving — 'Father Bother'

Episcopal minister and columnist Lester Kinsolving was denied renewal of his membership in the Senate and House daily press galleries by a special committee of his colleagues in 1977 after it was made public that he had accepted a total of 2,500 US dollars from Donald de Keiffer, the Washington lobbyist representing the South African Government, as payment for Kinsolving's pro-South African editorial voice. But according to *The Star*, 6 August 1979, he had also been allotted some R21,000 of stock in various companies by Donald de Keiffer which allowed him to attend five annual meetings of companies in 1975 and a further eight in 1976.

Until 1977 Kinsolving had been a White House correspondent for WAVA AM and FM, an all-news radio station in suburban Arlington, Virginia, and was known as 'Father Bother' by certain White House colleagues because of his abrasive questioning of officials.

In February 1975 he went on a subsidized 10-day trip to South Africa and returned to write an attack on a Christian organization which has since been banned and which Mr Kinsolving maintained had misrepresented the political prisoner situation. Since 1977 he has been employed on two papers of the Panax Newspaper chain, the company owned by John McGoff.

After promising not to take part in shareholders' meetings while he held press credentials, Lester Kinsolving regained his admission to Congressional press galleries and then, in a pattern so often repeated in this narrative, announced that he had left the Episcopal Church in disgust to serve an independent parish.

Kinsolving was just one of many lobbyists recruited by the DOI at the peak of its drive to reach all the influential segments of American society. As reported in *The Star*, 6 August 1977, an examination of the Justice Department files shows that the South African Information Department had more personnel in Washington at one time than any other country except the Soviet Union. One of these lobbyists, and the most expensive, was Donald de Keiffer, hired by Eschel Rhoodie in 1976 to mount several sensitive and strategic secret operations for which he was paid at least 397,245 US dollars for 18 months work — at the rate of 50 US dollars an hour. For three years he worked closely with the New York based public relations firm Sidney Baron. Figures filed by them in terms of the US Foreign Agents Act, filed in the Internal Security Section Registration Unit of the Department of Justice in Washington, show that Baron and de Keiffer between them received fees totalling 1,981,652 US dollars in the three years of their contract with the DOI.

Both undertook to promote the exchange of visits between influential South Africans and Americans in the business, communications and learning sectors and to supply corrective information to the media. Though they were not directly involved with the CLSA, their advice was sought on the North American tour and the CLSA sponsors also have their own contacts with de Keiffer who was aware of what was going on.

Internecine Warfare

Despite the work of paid sponsors, the expertise of the official South African public relations system and the information collecting and monitoring services of the South African Embassy, preparations for the CLSA tour were problematic.

All the sponsors who had been asked to help were highly volatile characters. They were just as likely to go off prematurely as to fail to go off at all.

Dr Joost Sluis was listed, in early editions of the public pamphlets, as a sponsor in California. He was head of Christian Cause International, a right-wing organization, but had not agreed to be listed, and he had to be removed and replaced by Dr W S McBirnie of the Community Churches of America, best known as the founder of American Christian Cause to combat the gay activist movement.

The Rev Colonel John Hinkel suddenly became sensitive about the use of his old army title in connection with a 'religious' organization.

Then the US Justice Department, which had been consulted by Colonel Hinkel about whether the speakers coming from South Africa should register as foreign agents, sent all the sponsors a warning. They received a letter which said, 'It has recently come to the attention of this Department that you may be engaged in activities on behalf of the Christian League of Southern Africa which may require your registration pursuant to the Foreign Agents Registration Act. Since meetings between your foreign principals, the Christian League of Southern Africa, and groups in your geographic area are scheduled to begin on October 10, 1978, your registration is due in this office on or before that date.'

The purpose of the Foreign Agents Registration Act, first enacted in 1938, and revised several times since, seemed simple enough: identification of the sources of foreign propaganda.

Several of the sponsors complained bitterly. Nevertheless those who were being paid to help, such as Colonel Hinkel, had to register. The touring speakers also had to register 'because their purpose in coming to the United States is not strictly religious but also involves political matters.' Even the intervention of right-wing senator Jesse Helms failed to resolve the problem.[17]

When the League's travelling circus went on the road in the United States, the results were disappointing in view of their powerful backing. The NCC's Africa Committee[18] representative said that apart from flyers and leaflets sent in by friends, it had had no feedback. The United Methodist Board of Global Ministries office thought their impact was nil, because they spoke mostly to people who were already on their side.

The newspapers mainly ignored them except when they were banned from speaking at Duke University in Durham, North Carolina, on the grounds that it would promote 'white supremacist ideology'. Dr Paul Mickey, a close colleague of Fred Shaw, is Associate Professor of Pastoral Theology at Duke. He is a frequent visitor to Europe and has been a delegate at Christian Affirmation Campaign meetings; he was also one of the interim committee delegates of the International Christian Network (see Chapter 4), listed as Vice-Chairman. Like Keyser he appears to be a member of the 'Good News' pressure group within the United Methodist Church, and gained some publicity when he publicly appealed for the resignation of the church's entire Women's Division staff because of their criticism of Rhodesia's internal settlement.

In response to criticism of CLSA's racist message, Father Arthur Lewis, one of the speakers, claimed that the group 'is not connected with any government, any political party, or any political party line'. Father Lewis charged that 'someone is spreading the word that we're a right-wing group. This is simply not true'.

As an effort to launch a national Christian crusade to make the US Government ally itself with South Africa, the CLSA's initiative was a failure. However, Shaw claimed significant advances on the economic front. In the government-backed newspaper *The Citizen*, Shaw was reported as saying that he and his speakers had laid the foundations for tremendous new investment in South Africa — running potentially into many billions of dollars. In the United States, Father Lewis had claimed to be on a religious mission: 'We are merely Christians and we want to get our story across.'

Conclusion

In itself, the CLSA has minimal impact in the United States; however, it has close contacts with organizations many times more powerful who promote the white supremacist message through their own 'Christian' organizations and media. Religion, wealth and the possibility of investment, mercenary violence and the apartheid message for white racists in the American South are inextricably intermingled. The South Africans, evidently, have decided that it is well worthwhile associating with right-wingers who have little credibility in their own communities, because of the money, the media access and the organizational muscle which they offer. The Department of Information and its front organizations may have been exposed, but the alliance between the South African Government and the American far right is still very much alive. The land of apartheid has become the promised land for white supremacists in the United States.

References

1. *The Star,* Johannesburg, 22 December 1979.

2. *New African,* November 1979.

3. Paper by ICCR, 1979.

4. Space Research Corp and its two top officials pleaded guilty on 25 March 1980, to charges that they exported arms and artillery to South Africa in violation of US law and a United Nations embargo. This was the culmination of a 23-month government investigation of the munitions firm. It was also revealed that South Africa owns 20 per cent of the company as a result of a 10 million US dollar investment in the company in 1977. Whether this is one of the un-revealed slush fund projects is still a matter of speculation.

5. John Stockwell, *In Search of Enemies: A CIA Story* (New York: Norton, 1978).

6. 'An up-town Ku Klux Klan', John Thayer, *The Farthest Shores of Politics*, NY 1977.

7. *The Star,* Johannesburg, 19 April 1980.

8. Karen Rothmyer, 'The McGoff Grab', *Columbia Journalism Review*, November/December 1979.

9. *Indianapolis Star,* 23 and 24 March 1980.

10. *Encounter,* August 1977.

11. Atlanta Journal and Contribution, 13 May 1979.

12. *Apostles of Discord* by Ralph Lord Ray, The Beacon Press, Boston 1953, see also Daniel Bell (ed) *The Radical Right*, Doubleday, 1963.

13. 'How the Communists use Religion' and 'Collectivism in the Churches' available from the Church League of America, 422 North Prospect Street, Wheaton, Illinois 60187.

14. The NCCC is the National Council of the Churches of Christ, the ecumenical organization of American churches, the US equivalent of the British Council of Churches.

15. US News and World Report, 24 September 1979.

16. Atlanta Constitution, 23 May 1979.

17. Jesse Helms has a long record of opposition to civil rights and racial equality. He has been active in all attempts to lift US restrictions against the régimes in Rhodesia and South Africa.

18. See earlier footnote in this chapter.

8. The Rulers of Darkness

The individuals mentioned in this text all propagate a conspiracy theory of history. Bernard Smith in the *Church Times*, 1 July 1977, accused 'that great fraternity of Socialists, Communists, Trotskyists, and nameless radicals who have been working with such dedication over the past 25 years to diminish our political liberties, destroy our patriotism (which has gloriously survived) and to ferment class-hatred as a preparation for revolution'.

Fred Shaw in *Encounter*, June 1979, points to the 'deliberately planned' and secret experiences of 'the Club of Rome in concert with the World Council of Churches and other related bodies, to bring about a new breed of humanity that will accept a One World Community with a single economic, social and religious basis'.

Father Arthur Lewis is 'against the rulers of darkness in this world' (December 1977, RCG newsletter) and he explains:

> 'Quite literally we are up against Satan himself: against the rulers of darkness of this world, against spiritual wickedness in high places. Satan has his tools in East and West: the Russian ambassador in Lusaka, Mr Solodovnikov, is the chief planner of the Marxist take-over of Southern Africa, as the Foreign Office is the author of "sanctions" and the lie of "illegality". Satan too has his tools in the WCC and in the financiers who provide the sinews of world communism.' (RCG newsletter No 6, 1979)

Dr Eschel Rhoodie was 'against a conspiracy whose purpose it is to bring all mankind under a total and centralised control' (*Paper Curtain*).

Richard Hofstadter, in an influential collection of essays called *The Paranoid Style in American Politics and other essays* on the conspiratorial mind describes the style of the conspiracy theorist as 'paranoid'. In the American context he discusses people and movements on the extreme right wing politically, who 'believe that we have lived for a generation in the grip of a vast conspiracy'. 'The distinguishing thing about the paranoid style,' he writes, 'is not that its exponents see

150

conspiracies or plots here and there in history but that they regard a "vast" or "gigantic" conspiracy as the motive force in historical events. History is a conspiracy, set in motion by demonic forces of almost transcendent power, and what is felt to be needed to defeat it is not the usual methods of political give-and-take, but an all-out crusade.'

Michael Billig in his analysis of the social psychology of the National Front, *Fascists*, published in 1978, has an invaluable summary of the way the myth of a world conspiracy has arisen. We are indebted to his research in this field.

'The themes in the present-day conspiracy theories,' he writes, 'can be traced back to the myths which developed round masonic sects and secret societies in the eighteenth century, and in particular around one society — Adam Weishaupt's Illuminati, founded in 1776. Two classic works, claiming to disclose the hidden conspiracies behind the French Revolution, laid the basis for the conspiracy tradition: August de Barruel's *Mémoires pour servir à l'histoire du Jacobinisme*, whose first volumes were published in 1797, and John Robinson's *Proofs of a conspiracy against all the religions and governments of Europe, carried on in the secret meetings of Free Masons, Illuminati and Reading Societies*, published in the same year and which established the conspiracy tradition in Britain.'

These first conspiracy theories set out to expose the evil forces behind Jacobinism, the fierce egalitarian movement underpinning the French Revolution, but since that time conspiracy theories have been enlisted to support a variety of causes.

In the America of the 30s, Gerald Winrod's deeply fundamentalist Defenders of the Christian Faith linked contemporary Communism with a Jesuit-Jewish conspiracy and accused all three of combining to destroy fundamentalist Protestantism. There were Protestant traitors too, since the 'Modernists' of the Federal Council of Churches (the forerunner of the National Council of Churches of Christ) were in effect Judaised Protestants. It followed that liberal Protestant churches were seen as fronts for Jewish Communists.

In the same period, a gifted orator with a wide radio following, Father Charles Coughlin, led a pro-Nazi organization called the National Union for Social Justice. Coughlin denounced Jews, international bankers, the League of Nations, communism. His weekly newspaper *Social Justice* reprinted *The Protocols of the Learned Elders of Zion* and defended the persecution of

151

Jews by Nazis and fascists. His political career was halted when America became involved in the war against Hitler and his Archbishop threatened that he would be defrocked unless he shut up shop.

A parallel movement of the 30s was that of the Silver Shirts, an openly fascist organization founded by William Dudley Pelley who wanted dictatorship, the suppression of trade unions and the use of violence to attain power. Pelley was a fundamentalist Protestant. His scheme for reorganizing the American economy was called The Christian Commonwealth (labels can never be trusted in the conspiracy world). Pelley applauded Father Coughlin's Social Justice movement but went even further in blaming the Jews and their world-wide conspiracies for all the problems of society, the depression, communism and the spread of immorality. The themes developed in these years are still part of the conspiracy language of today.

The current heirs to these movements in Britain today are the National Front and its extremist offshoots, the League of St George and the British Movement, but they are by no means the only groups. There are others whose literature is spread in the States and in Europe by the mail order catalogues of Bloomfield Books and others. A list of some of the main suppliers of conspiracy material in Britain is given in an appendix (see p 180).

In recent years South African affairs have provided a rich source for conspiracy theory. They spring from a background in which a white minority population is holding on to power and privilege at the expense of a large black population; the special inherited characteristics of the Afrikaners, which include a religious faith and culture drawn from a unique interpretation of the Bible making the Afrikaners a chosen race and thus justifying apartheid; the Broederbond, a secret society with Nazi characteristics and sympathies whose members control the key posts in the South African Government, in public affairs and industry; a crisis of identity amongst Christians; a pathological fear of communism enshrined as part of Afrikaner nationalist ideology and used as an excuse for a comprehensive system of repressive legislation which makes a mockery of freedom and imposes censorship on any published material critical of the system. Add to these the economic power bestowed by natural resources in minerals which form one of the biggest strategic reserves of scarce metals in the world.

The apartheid government, while accusing the world of conspiring against it, is itself engaging in a vast conspiracy on its own terms. A 'crusade' with a £33 million budget of secret money to challenge the 'sinister' powers which threaten its way of life.

Pressure groups such as the Christian League of Southern Africa and the Rhodesian Christian Group, who were fighting apartheid South Africa's battle before Dr Rhoodie's Grand Design got going and funds for new projects became available, were already deeply committed to the cause and were not likely to be diverted by the revelations of a huge public scandal. Indeed, this has proved to be the case. Fred Shaw has repeatedly shrugged off Muldergate as of no great moment. Occasionally, however, the attempt to give focus to abstract 'demonic' forces goes awry.

In November 1978, the prestigious American paper *The Christian Science Monitor* published a report by its South African correspondent June Goodwin in which she said she had been told by Mrs Fred Shaw, whose husband was then on a lecture tour of the States, that the SACC had received R5 million from overseas in 1977 and that the money was used 'to distribute kits with directions on how to make bombs'. Mrs Shaw added that the League did not have documentation on the kits but 'we are busy with our documentation' she said. Fred Shaw, asked to comment, denied that his wife made the statement but *The Christian Science Monitor* reporter remained in no doubt about it. In a report in the South African *Sunday Tribune*, 12 November 1978, the SACC was said to be considering legal action against the CLSA following Mrs Shaw's statement. No supportive documents were ever found.

Two of the contributors to *Encounter*, the newspaper of the CLSA, are Ivor Benson and Bill Chalmers. Ivor Benson is a veteran journalist-writer whose fanatical support for apartheid goes beyond that of most Afrikaners. His main contribution to the conspiracy theme is his book *The Worldwide Conspiracy* which is on the National Front's recommended list. Benson is not only a regular contributor to *Encounter* but is frequently quoted in Donald Martin's newssheet *On Target*. This is a sample:

'Globally, South Africa is in precisely the same situation as countries like Paraguay, Chile, Taiwan and several others which are holding out for national self-determination against a conspiracy whose purpose is to bring all mankind under total and centralised control.'

(*On Target*, 3 November 1979)

153

Bill Chalmers, organizer of Religious Affairs on the Broeder-bond-controlled South African Broadcasting Corporation, is the best known English-speaking apologist for apartheid as 'Christian' ideology. He is the man who has ultimate censorship of the apartheid media and ensures that no word repudiating the system is allowed. He has been criticized for giving an undue proportion of available airtime to Fred Shaw and for sacking a young producer of his programme 'Crossroads' for refusing to include an interview with Shaw in the programme.

In 1979, Chalmers was at the centre of controversy over a booklet he wrote entitled *The Conspiracy of Truth*. The booklet alleged a world-wide communist-inspired conspiracy sponsored by the power of 'International Finance, a machinery developed by Jews, but willingly adopted by Westerns'.

In one of the most recent copies of *Encounter* (January 1980) Fred Shaw in a front page editorial expands the idea of conspiracy.

'All through the ages the forces of darkness have sought to enslave mankind, most often parading under the disguise of liberty and freedom. Precisely at the times when men have considered themselves to be secure, free and prosperous, have they in fact been most vulnerable. Those forces so clearly described and often attributed to the "Illuminati" are not imaginary — but neither can they be defined and limited to recognizable man-made institutions. They belong to Satan himself . . .'

The writing and preaching of Father Arthur Lewis, the Anglican missionary who became a senator in Ian Smith's Rhodesian parliament, illustrates how the language of Christianity can be used.

Yearning for an imagined past in Africa in the spurious social harmony of a colonial society, he sees himself paddling barefooted across sun-dappled streams in the search of souls to convert, a faithful black servant at his heels. In the villages the black people will come round like happy and disciplined children to listen to the word of the white man's God. But the winds of change were already blowing through Rhodesia when Lewis was posted from East Africa and his mission there has been one long confrontation with his colleagues who faced and sometimes encouraged the emergence of black political consciousness, while Lewis feared it.

He had to cope with the stand of politically conscious mission-educated young men and women who rebelled against the paternal role of the old type of mission. Unable to adjust, he seems to have felt an increasing sense of martyrdom. As colonial administrations gave way to independent African regimes across the whole of Africa, and the pressure grew on Rhodesia itself, the pressure on Lewis also grew.

If a man's writing is any indication of his state of mind, Lewis's raw, nervy, blood-soaked prose might be seen as evidence. He could not explain his own worsening relations with Africans and with Christian colleagues. More and more he seems to have sought justification and perhaps sanity in the comfort of conspiracy. As the years went by this conspiracy became focused on the spread of Marxism; the sharpness and gloom of his apocalyptic vision of a civilization betrayed has increased steadily in recent years as racial tension and conflict in the southern cone of Africa has grown.

Two of the classics constantly recommended in National Front publications are Nesta Webster's *World Revolution* (first published in 1921) and her *Secret Societies* (1924). The former is described in NF book lists as 'perhaps the best documented history of the political left and its conspiratorial origins', and the latter as 'the standard authority on the most important secret societies undermining civilizations and Christianity in the last 2000 years'. Both of these are advertised in Donald Martin's Bloomfield Books list.

A K Chesterton, the first chairman of the National Front, credited Ms Webster as one of the most important influences on his thought. Chesterton's *The New Unhappy Lords* is one of four works in the Bloomfield catalogue by this South African whose career, as a writer and political activist, started in the 1930s when he became a leading light in Oswald Mosley's British Union of Fascists and editor of its paper *Blackshirt*. *The New Unhappy Lords* is described as 'an exposure of the power behind politics in the modern world'. It was first published in 1965 and by 1975 was in its second printing of a fourth revised edition. According to Michael Billig in his book *Fascists*, it is primarily an outline of the 'world conspiracy' of this century. The National Front recommend it as essential reading and praise Chesterton for doing more than anyone else to understand 'the network of conspiracies' underlying British politics.

Chesterton was a close friend of Eric Butler, the veteran Australian right-winger and anti-semitic pamphleteer from whom Donald Martin derived his early training and inspiration (see chapter 2).

On 15 February 1975, Donald Martin wrote his supporters a letter on British League of Rights notepaper which included the following paragraphs:

> 'I am happy to be able to announce to you an entirely new and unique scheme of co-operation between the League and Britons Publishing Company — neither of us is surrendering or altering our identity in any way, since we both operate complementary services which will be to the advancement of the common cause — to give you and the general public a steady improvement in our services, and the prospect of a firm base for future expansion.

> 'Britons Publishing Company under the direction of Mr Timothy Tindal-Robertson will give us access to a sympathetic publisher who can help us with certain printing and at the same time provide a co-operative service with respect to our general list of books.'

The significance of this will only be apparent to those who know the history of Britons. In the early 1920s Britons Publishing Company was the brainchild of H H Beamish, an Englishman who later emigrated to Rhodesia where he was interned during the Second World War for his pro-Nazi activities. His motto was 'Britain for the Britons'. The objectives of his organization were 'to protect the Birthright of Britons and to eradicate Alien influences from our politics and industries' and 'to assist white patriotic organizations all over the world with information on the Communist, World Government and the Multi-Racial conspiracy, and the work of Subversive Secret Societies'.

In 1920 Britons took over the publishing of *The Protocols of the Learned Elders of Zion*, the most infamous anti-semitic text. Since then they have produced some 80 editions of the translation by V E Marsden.

Throughout the 1930s and up to the death of Beamish in 1947, Britons published and distributed all kinds of anti-semitic and conspiracy books and papers. After the war the Beamish headquarters in London was sold to Colin Jordan and Britons Publishing Company moved to Devon and became an anti-communist business. It was run by a disciple of Nesta Webster and friend of Arnold Leese, Anthony Gittens. After Gittens' death in 1973 it was taken over by Timothy Tindal-Robertson, a Catholic traditionalist. In 1977 Britons ceased to trade and a new print house was formed called the Augustine Publishing Company whose primary objective 'is to uphold traditional Roman Catholic doctrines and uncover the true nature and extent of the crisis in the Church precipitated by the onslaught of Modernism since Vatican Council II'.

Augustine's book lists have been trimmed of mainly conspiratorial works unless written by Catholics like Father Denis Fahey (an Irish theologian who argued that Jews now controlled Russia and were in league with the Devil in a conspiracy to conquer the world). It now features many works supportive of the Tridentine Mass movement of Archbishop Lefèbvre. This movement, critics have been warned, attracts a circus following with a fascist mentality. Lefèbvre's own dictum 'Justice, Order, Discipline, Authority,' which he is fond of repeating, has a familiar ring. Augustine also published a number of laudatory booklets on the Tridentine Mass by Michael Davies, a member of the Christian Affirmation Campaign.

The Bloomfield-Britons project announced in 1975 never materialized. Enquiries for overtly political or conspiracy theory works at Augustine's address (the same as Britons Publishing) are now referred to Donald Martin and Bloomfield Books which also lists much of the John Birch Society and other American right-wing texts which formerly belonged to Britons.

The Bloomfield book list is regularly boosted in the Christian Affirmation Campaign newsletters. It features Bernard Smith's *The Fraudulent Gospel* which is sandwiched between *The Naked Capitalist* by Skousen W Cleon, a rabid American conspiracy writer and Social Credit Secretariat's 'anonymous' booklet *Zimunism*, which fuses together the Zionist-Communist conspiracy to destroy the world money system.

Smith sees Marxist subversion in every programme of social change. He sees a conspiracy by a small committee of intellectuals to lead the world's churches by their noses. The WCC has been occupied by a 'higher diabolic force' and he identifies Marxism with Satan and the anti-Christ with the WCC. The influence of Nesta Webster's revival of the medieval conception of the Devil can perhaps be discerned.

Pawns in the Game by William Guy Carr, an Englishman who settled in Canada and lived there until his death in 1959, was first published in Toronto in 1956 and is now in the Bloomfield book list. It deals with the conspiracy theory in the 20th century. Carr wrote:

'History repeats itself because there has been perfect continuity of purpose in the struggle which has been going on since the beginning of time between the forces of Good and Evil to decide whether the rule of the Almighty God shall prevail, or whether the world shall literally go to the Devil. The issue is as simple as that.'

Carr believed that Jesus was ordered to be killed by the 18th century 'Illuminati' and that they were behind every revolutionary movement from the French Revolution to the present. He said that they also 'use Communism today as their manual of action to further their secret plan for ultimate world destruction. Some of their other accomplices are internationalists, World Federalists, international bankers, Zionists and integrationists'.

Carr's ideas were taken a step further by Robert Welch, the American who founded the John Birch Society in 1958. Welch credited the 'Illuminati' with the master-minding of the communist conspiracy in the 19th century and with being behind it ever since. He called them The Insiders. The Insiders, according to Welch, were behind both World Wars, the Russian Revolution and the spread of communism after World War II. They engineered the collapse of the colonial empires and the development of the United Nations.

Enough has been said to show the influence of the conspiracy theory on the motley collection of characters mentioned in this book. In a sense this influence has fortified them against rational argument and judgement. The subject has a vast literature of its own for those who wish to undertake the necessary research.

The current period of ominous and apocalyptic events and trends may increase the numbers of people yearning for a simple way of understanding what is going on in the world. And disillusionment with rational arguments may enhance the appeal of the conspiracy theory. Indeed, to some extent this is already happening. In the United States *The Conspiracy Digest*, a pseudo-academic journal, offers a focus for just such an interest.

In Britain, the existence of specialist catalogues and rightwing book clubs points to a possible resurgence of interest.

Running through all this literature is a contempt for democratic social structures and a yearning for autocratic solutions to political problems. It has been repeatedly demonstrated by contemporary historians and commentators how the bogey of a Jewish conspiracy of world domination with its allies in international finance and in communism was the heart of Nazi ideology.

The holocaust was the result. All the booksellers whose

stock-in-trade is racialism and conspiracy are encouraging a Nazi revival. The organizations and people in the text are not Nazis, but in the event of a Nazi revival, they may well be the ideological seed-bed from which such a revivial would grow.

9. Suggestions for Reflection/ Discussion/Action

The underlying thread of this report has been the existence of a Christian underworld in Britain and in many other countries. It consists of groups, sects and individuals on the fringes of established religion and politics. It has probably always existed in some form and was recently under pressure from a powerful group of politicians in South Africa. Between 1974 and 1978 especially — the period in which some of these activities have been exposed — they plotted a ruthless campaign for what they saw as the survival of their way of life. The campaign was secret and the objective was to manipulate public opinion in Britain and in many other parts of the world. It attempted to buy control of influential areas of the international media and developed a strategy to try and destroy the broad-based Christian consensus against apartheid. It took on the World Council of Churches as a main target, and called upon likely and unlikely allies to help.

This book was written to alert people generally and Christians in particular to the ways in which this campaign has progressed. It has not been an easy task. The Muldergate investigations and the exposure of many secret projects financed by South Africa may have neutralized some of the energy which fired the world campaign, but the many small groups and people who did the leg-work are still active.

In the process of trying to tread a path through a maze of material we are only too aware that it has not been possible to expand on many of the fundamental issues raised in the text. A short list of further reading is suggested at the end of this book together with a short list of organizations which are working for constructive solutions to the problems of southern Africa.

One of the themes running through these pages has been the evil of racism. Racism creates fear and violence. The condemnation of the system of apartheid in South Africa by Christians all over the world and co-ordinated in particular by the words and actions of the WCC, partly explains the bitter attack on the churches by the South African government both directly and through its massive propaganda campaign. Behind it, however, are many individuals and groups who have co-operated and worked along with this campaign.

The individual who wishes to challenge such an evil needs to be fully aware of the current thinking on racism and the churches' response to it, especially in Britain. Opportunities should be sought to discuss the issues in church and community gatherings. The simple pamphlet *Christianity and Race* by John Hick, available from AFFOR, is very helpful and it is also useful to read the BCC's study pamphlet *The New Black Presence in Britain* and the special pack of materials prepared by the Board of Deputies of British Jews about the National Front which says more about the mechanics of racial hatred in a short space than anything else available.

The BCC's Community and Race Relations Unit have a catalogue of materials and schedule of projects. Christians Against Racism and Fascism (CARAF) also prepares educational materials and holds meetings in many parts of the country.

Another of the underlying themes has been the response to 'terrorism'. The tragic civil war in Rhodesia generated hatred and brutalities on both sides; often these were distorted in the official media and by partisan reporters. In particular, the well-intentioned but sometimes clumsily publicized humanitarian programmes, supported by the World Council of Churches and other church agencies, aroused quite disproportionate hostility. The Programme to Combat Racism became a kind of white man's bogey. The campaign against it, orchestrated by the South African security and information departments at one time seriously threatened to disrupt the fund-raising efforts of the churches for development programmes all over the world.

The story of the involvement of the churches in the issue of segregation and the destructive evil of racism is told in *A Small Beginning* by Elizabeth Adler (World Council of Churches 1974) which assesses the first five years of the Programme to Combat Racism up to 1973 and puts it in its historical perspective. A pack of written papers and PCR project details, bringing the story up to date, is available from the CRRU (see addresses below). *Shalom and Combat*, a personal struggle against racism by Albert van den Heuvel (World Council of Churches) is an account of 20 years of ecumenical experience in meeting the problems of racism and violence.

Many of us are daily bombarded with publicity sheets, pamphlets and appeals. A high proportion of these go straight into the wastepaper basket, but occasionally one is intriguing or frightening enough to keep and read. How does one assess it? It is important to weigh up and authenticate all printed matter.

The first thing is to find out where it came from. If it is from an organization or an individual then what do they represent? In many countries all printed material has to be identifiable by law. This makes it more difficult for an anonymous slander or libel to be published without it being tracked down. But there are still ways of getting round the law. Some pressure groups who prefer anonymity hide themselves behind P O box numbers. Is this done for efficiency in dealing with the expected response? Is it because the group or organization is too small or too new to have its own office? Is it something to do with the content of the printed material itself? If the last, why cannot the sender be open about the origin of the material?

What does the sending organization represent — if anything? It may be a substantial or even a prestigious body, such as a well known charity or a substantial political or consumer group. It may, on the other hand, be only a window dressing. This report has described so-called groupings which fit the latter description.

Cheap printing technology has enabled groups with slender resources to print and circulate newsletters or bulletins at minimal cost. The technique of appealing to the grassroots by the circulation of strongly worded appeals and the distribution of handbills in the street is one that has for long been the prerogative of the political left, but it has now been adopted by the right. Editorial content is borrowed and copied from other journals at home or abroad, some of it extremely scurrilous. One reason mentioned previously for the popularity of selective mailings by racist societies is in order to avoid prosecution. A wide use of grandiose or innocuous-sounding names is another tactic to disguise sometimes quite sinister motives. There is also the seductive appeal of receiving, as one group tells the would-be member, 'highly confidential memos in plain sealed envelopes to keep them informed . . .'

A favourite trick of those who wish to influence opinion is to choose an important-sounding title for a one-person cause. A gloss on this is to set up a number of organizations, all of which are different faces of the same body. A precise example can be taken from the technique of the Unification Church in the UK. Its formal title is the Holy Spirit Association for the Unification of World Christianity. It is popularly referred to as The Moonies. The organization operates under a number of other names: Sun Myung Moon Foundation; International Cultural Foundation; International Federation for Victory Over Communism; International One World Crusade; International Brass Band; Federation for World Peace and Unification; Unified Family Singers; New Hope Singers; International New Hope Crusade Choir; New Life Singers International; Council for Unified Research and Education; Cartographers Crafts Ltd; Freedom Leadership Foundation; God's Light Infantry; The Weekly Religion; Carnation Appeal; The College for Research in Principle; Kensington Gardens Arts Society; Inter-University Cultural Organization; World Unity Programme; New Hope Crusade; United Family Enterprises Ltd; Creative Community Projects; Go-World Brass Band; New Horizons; Tongues of Fire; Ocean Fresh Ltd; Little Angels — now called National Folk Ballet (Korea).

The National Front in the United Kingdom has used fanciful names to obtain bookings in public halls or rooms over pubs. A few which are known include The Mid-Kent Model Engineering Society, The Riverside Angling Club (RACE), The South-East Veterans Association.

Another trick is to choose a title which sounds similar to a well-known and reputable organization in order to create an association in the mind of the reader or at least cause a confusion of identity. An example of the latter is the anonymous British racist who has been publishing anti-semitic broadsheets as coming from the British Board of Deputies and using a box number address — an obvious attempt to muddle readers into thinking it comes from the Board of Deputies of British Jews, a charity defending the rights of Jews. Then again, the Rhodesia Christian Group, which is affiliated to the CLSA and represented a tiny body of white supremacists in what was formerly Rhodesia, could be confused with the Rhodesian (now Zimbabwean) Christian Council which represents a wide spectrum of denominational and missionary concern. The Christian League of Southern Africa has a name similar to Christian Concern for Southern Africa, a Catholic anti-apartheid agency in London which is particularly involved with achieving social justice in business and industry. And so on.

Words with particular and accepted associations often conceal the nature of a group. Christian, Crusade, Cross, Church in a title do not necessarily indicate that the group is committed to

163

the doctrines preached by Christ. On the contrary, some of the most racist and politically violent groups in the United States use these words. For example, Christian Defence League in the States is an armed group preaching racial intolerance, closely tied in with the Minutemen and the Ku Klux Klan. The 'Unification' Church is not a Christian Church. *The Cross and the Flag* is a Klansman-type newspaper.

It is not simply a question of confusing titles. The use of words has to be closely scrutinized. Certain words are now incapable of clear definition because they have been put to service in so many conflicting causes. For example, in some circles the word 'liberal' is a term of abuse, but the Liberal Party in Britain is a respected middle-of-the-road political party. When challenged by a fellow South African parliamentarian about using the euphemism of 'separate development', when what he meant was the more brutal word 'apartheid', Dr Andreas Treuricht, the hardline Verkampte Afrikaner politician quoted a Chinese proverb: 'a beloved child has many names'.

Question the sources of information in news reports or pamphlets. Look at the press critically. What is known about editorial policy? Is the article or report attributed? The integrity of named journalists can easily be checked. Material from government sources — especially countries where censorship or reporting restrictions exist — has to be looked at sceptically. Bias, in the political sense, can be of the right or of the left. If you know the source, it will be possible for you to judge the objectivity of most journalism. The smaller and specialist journals are often hungry for copy and may not have the resources to investigate submitted materials. Watch out for publicity handouts or press releases republished verbatim. Develop a questioning attitude.

Material or letters from private organizations published in the religious or secular press should be evaluated. Do not be misled by fancy organizational labels, ask what or who they represent.

Watch out for loaded reporting of events in the papers, radio or TV. Watch out for provocative language designed to stir up racial hatred. Watch out for dirty tricks. All groups or causes use the letter columns of newspapers to air their views and principles, but the National Front issues instructions to its members on how to do it and how to pen hoax and deceitful letters:

'Such letters need not directly advertise the fact that the writer is a NF member — indeed, depending on the game being played in any particular letter, the very opposite impression might usefully be given. NF members who have gained publicity as NF activists should adopt a nom-de-plume. Our phantom letter-writers must work overtime to put to the test that 'nice and respectable' multiracialism! On this theme letters should come from individuals who do not betray any party political "leanings".'[1]

Many examples are listed in Chapter·2. Learn to identify types of rhetoric. The executives of the Christian League of Southern Africa have a way of trying to turn words with a generally recognizable meaning on their heads. Fred Shaw, in an article on the great Christian gathering of SACLA organized in Pretoria in the summer of 1979 to bring together a wider cross-section of churches than ever before in South Africa, spoke of this being 'a terrifying experience' for conservative Afrikaners, which might induce them to make hasty concessions to bring about 'what ecumenicals call "reconciliation" '.[2]

Watch out for the emotive language of terrorism being used to describe the legitimate aspirations of freedom fighters against a repressive régime.

Do not accept at face value a declaration by any Christian movement or its representative that it has no political focus and that Christianity should not be concerned with politics. Some of the most adamant critics of the involvement of the churches in political issues are themselves deeply political, though denying it. In a sense, that is the underlying dimension of this text.

Beware of the line of argument which relates all history and all world events to a giant conspiracy of a small élite of power-hungry people — bankers, Jews, communists, Freemasons, the UN, the Bilderberg Conference, the World Council of Churches or whatever. There are of course conspiracies in all levels of society, but there is no evidence that we are all the victims of some remote and gigantic manipulation either of industrial magnates, secret societies of international Jews, or the KGB.

The increasingly bitter attacks on the churches has been met on the whole by a shrug of their collective shoulders. The churches took the attitude, not unreasonably, in the case of its individual critics, that if you ignore a problem long enough it may go away. The Gospel furthermore exhorts all Christians to love their enemies. This was fine until the former South African Department of Information spent hundreds of thousands of pounds on an international campaign to discredit the WCC and with it the member churches all over the world opposed to apartheid and supportive of the Africans' struggle for equal rights in southern Africa.

The steady seepage of unanswered propaganda in a widespread campaign, using all kinds of channels of communication to reach grassroots Christian communities, dismayed many of the faithful. Now, at least, the mechanics of this orchestrated campaign are understood and the critics can be challenged.

Make yourself responsible for finding out and keeping informed about the complex issues on which Christians need to have a say. Take part in church or community groups where such things are discussed. Make your views heard. Find a practical way of getting involved.

We are not the first generation which has found that the fanatic who takes the scriptures literally, if selectively, and is blind to their historical perspective, is the scourge of any sort of practical adjustment of Christian values in line with scientific advance and social trends. To these people, what happens in 'their' world is often utterly irreconcilable with what happens in the 'real' world. Rational argument has no bearing on their beliefs because the world they know is a world of make-believe, of unreason.

References

1. *Hackney Gazette*, 23 April 1976; *Wembley and Brent Times*, 4 February 1977.
2. *Encounter*, June 1979.

POSTSCRIPT

The text of 'Beyond the Pale' was written almost two years ago at the height of the South African attempt to buy influence in the rest of the world and to challenge a growing Christian consensus that racism, as practised by the white minority in South Africa, was one of the greatest evils of our time.

Between 1973 and 1978, some £35 million was put at the disposal of the South African Department of Information for the activation of a list of some 180 secret projects. The official Erasmus Commission investigation in 1978 and 1979 revealed many of these projects, but at least 56 remained hidden. Further detective work by the press and by other organizations who suspected they were unwitting targets of one or more of these projects exposed more secrets. Others still remain obscure. It seemed likely that these continued in the care of the reorganized information department now called ISSA, or under the umbrella of the Ministry of Defence.

On 29 March 1980, the Johannesburg *Sunday Express* published details of a contract drawn up and signed in Pretoria on 1 June 1979, by Mr Vlok Delport, acting on behalf of the Division for Secret Projects of the former Department of Information and the Rev Fred Shaw, chairman of the Christian League of Southern Africa. In terms of the contract the League undertook to infiltrate all the English churches affiliated to the SACC 'the largest Christian church body in South Africa and to influence both white and black churchmen to withdraw their membership of the SACC, and the World Council of Churches, to which the SAAC is affiliated'.

R340,000 was to be paid to the CLSA out of taxpayers' money to enable it to carry out this task. Amongst other things specified in the contract were the following:

   a) that five prominent church leaders from overseas should be brought to South Africa to help influence local churchmen to withdraw their membership from the SACC and WCC.

   b) that the Rev Fred Shaw should undertake visits to various countries, including Britain and the United States, to propagate the ideals of the League as opposed to those of the SAAC, on radio, TV, newspapers and at seminars organised for that purpose.

   c) that the League arrange meetings in South Africa to seek support for its campaign to break the influence of the SACC over its member churches; and devote at least 12 editions of its official newsletter 'Encounter' and at least five editions of its European journal 'Vox Africana' to the project. The League was also required to launch a similar campaign in Zimbabwe.

The campaign was carried out fully and the R340,000 paid out to the CLSA but the contract was ended in 1980.

As if to confirm the financial backing he received from the State, the Rev Fred Shaw instituted a claim for R260,000 against the Foreign Minister, Mr Pik Botha, and Mr Andries Engelbrecht, who was a senior official at the former Department of Information. The two men allegedly broke the terms of the secret contract in which there was a clause specifying that if there was a breach of confidence on either side, or if either party exposed the project publicly, the contract would be severed and the innocent party could sue the other for its losses.

The *Sunday Express* in a leader commented that it was a shattering blow to discover that a Government dedicated to cleaner administration should consider it acceptable to use taxpayers' money for a secret project to undermine a perfectly legal organisation representing many of the foremost churches in the land. It went on to call the project 'indefensible'. 'There could hardly be any plan more devious or disgraceful than this clandestine intrusion by the Government into the religious affairs of its citizens.' It also accused the Prime Minister of 'political cynicism of a high order' because he met an invited delegation from the SACC to exchange views about peaceful change in South Africa shortly after the Christian League project had been halted.

Days later the Foreign Minister issued secret documents to prove that the Christian League secret project was started by Dr Eschel Rhoodie and approved by Dr Connie Mulder on 13 March 1978, for the sum of R332,000. The document listing the League project as G11C stated that one of its aims was to rally support for South Africa against false representations made by the World Council of Churches, the SACC, the National Council of Churches (USA), the All Africa Conference of Churches, and the news media.

Mr Botha claimed to have evaluated secret projects for the first time on 28 March 1979, and to have questioned the continuation of funding the CLSA. It was decided however to keep it going and a contract was drawn up to formalise the situation, giving the Government the option of ending the contract on 31 March 1980. In the event this is what the Government decided to do.

On 13 March 1980, only two weeks earlier, the Rev Fred Shaw, giving evidence to the Steyn Commission into the mass media had denied that he was a Government agent or frontman and while admitting that the League had received secret Government funds, it was without his knowledge.

Further light on the Secret Projects list

Less than a week later the *Star* published details of 112 secret projects which were part of the original DOI list. Apparently the list was given the paper by hard-liners in the Nationalist Party trying to clear the names of colleagues forced to resign from office because of the Information scandal. The list contained 15 secret projects in the United Kingdom but there were many others. In publishing the list, however, the *Star* decided to black out many of the names until it could verify them independently. They come in a seven page letter from Dr Connie Mulder to Mr Owen Horwood, Minister of Finance, dated 3 May 1978:

G5 and 16D	. . . Germany and fellow-workers
G6	Club of Ten, London
G8A	Don de Kiefier and Associates, Washington
G8B	Liaison programme in Latin America
G8C and D	Liaison programmes in Germany
G8E	Special . . . liaison programme in USA, especially with regard to senators and academics
G11A and 11B	Ad hoc church actions; NGK special overseas education programme
G11C	Christian League of Southern Africa and actions in Britain and US
G11D	Church actions in Germany
G16F	. . . publisher, London
G18	Case Studies in Human Rights – central manuscript
G19	Institute for the Study of Plural Societies (Holland)
G20A to 20G	Special conferences in US, Germany, South Africa, London and France
G26P	Foreign Policy Research Institute, London
G27	Legal actions in the US, Britain, Netherlands and Germany
G32	Foreign guests of front organisations
G34A	Valiant Publications
G34E	SA Freedom Foundation
G35	Special South West African actions against SWAPO
G45	Foreign Affairs Association
G48	British Parliament members' visit to South Africa
G52	. . . London
G73	Management budget for British, French and South African operations including offices in Johannesburg, Paris and London
G88	. . . Association, Britain (60,000 members)
G89	Purchase of Review Investors, London and extension programme
G93	The establishment of . . . branch for South Africa as well as establishment of the head office in London and branch office in the US
G94	Actions in Scandinavia
G95	Special action programme for trade unions in Britain, Germany, Belgium and the US (nominal)
G96	Purchase of special space in newspapers and magazines in Europe, Australia and US by means of the so-called 'sailor' system whereby sympathetic journalists are involved.

Many of these were already known from Erasmus Commission published evidence. Much of the puzzle still remains, but there are many helpful leads. The national press in Britain and in Europe, sometimes so sharp in investigative journalism, has been noticeably passive in pursuing the answers. One wonders why!

Christian newspaper – a South African target

One piece of the puzzle was solved recently when the journalist Martin Bailey investigated how the Christian League had been involved in the attempt to purchase the weekly *Christian World*. The background of the plan is sketched at the end of Chapters Five and Six but Bailey probed deeper.

He relates how negotiations to purchase *Christian World* were begun in June 1979 while the paper was still appearing. These negotiations were set in motion by London solicitors Norton, Rose, Botterell and Roche, on instructions from Graeham Blainey, the London representative of the CLSA whose office at 53 Victoria Street (since demolished and its tenants dispersed) was shared with the International Christian Network (ICN).

168

In January 1980 it will be recalled the Rev Fred Shaw came to London accompanied by the Rev J F P Ebersohn and the Rev K Beukes. At the time of writing the first draft of 'Beyond the Pale' the author had no particular knowledge of the two Afrikaner Dominees visiting London who were apparently seeking to acquire audio-visual material from church and mission organisations to build their South African media project. The author then recalled that the original list of 41 signatures to the Berlin Declaration which launched the Fellowship of Confessing Christians (forerunner of the ICN) contained a strong group of signatories from South Africa. Testing these against the Broederbond listings in Wilkins and Strydom it became apparent that three out of six of these were members of the Broederbond. Readers are reminded that the militant wing of the Broederbond in World War II attempted to sabotage the Allies war effort against the Nazis. Many of its members who now control South African politics or business, were interned for the duration because of their pro-Nazi sympathies and may retain their old affiliations.

'ICN' according to the Rev John Mitchell in a newsletter dated June 1980 'is just a group of humble folk devoted to defending the faith'.

To return to the attempted purchase of the *Christian World*, it was not the CLSA but the ICN which was to publish it, but the two were at this time virtually inseparable and the ICN was dependent on CLSA funds, a large part of which were from the secret contract between Fred Shaw and the South African Government.

So in January 1980, John Mitchell moved from South Africa to Abingdon. The network's general committee met hurriedly at London Airport, confirmed Dr Peter Beyerhaus as Chairman, the Rev Matthew Calder, from New Zealand as Deputy Chairman and Dominee J F P Ebersohn as chairman of the South African branch. A separate committee was delegated to 'deal' with the possibility of taking over *Christian World*. The four members were Rev Fred Shaw, CLSA's American representative Dr Brenner, Dr Peter Beyerhaus, and London solicitor Graham Mather.

The owners of *Christian World* confirmed to Martin Bailey that they had been approached by Graham Mather to purchase the newspaper with his associates. The solicitors acting for Mather were Norton, Rose, Botterell and Roche.

Michael Palmer, a director of Christian Communications Trust, which owns the *Christian World*, told Bailey that he knew very little about the people behind the consortium which was hoping to buy the title. He had been told that their backers included the chairman of a bank and the rector of a City church, but the actual negotiations involved only two people, Graham Mather and Gervase Duffield*.

This is how Bailey's article concludes:

'Graham Mather, a solicitor and legal expert at the Institute of Directors, told Palmer on a number of occasions that there was no South African involvement in the group which had been hoping to buy the newspaper. But the Executive Secretary of International Christian Network has said that Mather is indeed a member of the organisation and sits on the committee set up to deal with the purchase.

'Gervase Duffield, the other person present at the negotiations, visited South Africa in 1978 on a trip sponsored by Dr Rhoodie's Department of Information. He claims that he is not a member of the International Christian Network. But the organisation's newsletter announced in January 1981 that while the Executive Secretary is away on a trip to South Africa, 'Duffield will answer telephone queries'. On his return Executive Secretary John Mitchell confirmed on the telephone that Duffield was indeed a member. Duffield admits he is 'the informal adviser to the Network on publications', but says he knows nothing about the financial side of the venture, and that it is 'a City Gent arrangement'.

'When the directors of *Christian World* recently learned about the growing evidence of South African money behind the consortium that was negotiating to purchase the newspaper, written assurances were sought that there was no South African involvement. Graham Mather did not provide these assurances, and the deal came to a

---

* Graham Mather had publicly denounced Christian Aid and other charities for supporting activities 'outside their legitimate objects' in an article in Free Nation of 6-19 July 1979 and he had ended 'Now it is for groups like the Freedom Association to keep a vigilant eye upon groups which seek the public's support as charities but in their operations further political ends'.

sudden end just a few weeks ago. The owners of *Christian World* are now convinced that they had almost become the innocent victim of a secret South African attempt to launch a new propoganda venture in Europe.'
(New Statesman, 29 May 1981)

Meanwhile on 31 March 1980, the South African Government ended its contract with the CLSA and effectively curtailed the expansionist dreams of that organisation and its offshoots.

In June 1980, the Rev John Mitchell, whose two year appointment commencing in January 1980, was slipping away, launched a six-page newsletter called *Monthly News Comment*. In it he writes of 'the frustrations and indecisions surrounding our journalistic hopes'. This newsletter with its decorated cover of flower patterns was published by Marsham Books of Appleford, the imprint owned by Gervase Duffield and credited to 'News Extra', the service which Duffield promotes to provide ready made inserts for parish magazines.

In November 1980 Mitchell sent out a special newsletter asking for funds – £5,000 to establish a monthly journal and £2,650 a month running costs.

In December 1980 came the next edition of *World Comment* which spoke of the problems of recent months when continuation of work became a major problem, but gifts and promises of further aid have allowed ICN to expand. It speaks of the development of videotape and colour slide programmes and of possible satellite links 'to beam radio and TV programmes to strategic areas'. It also announces the resignation of Fred Shaw from the ICN.

In March 1981 there was a further *World Comment* which devotes most of its limited space to pinning ICN's difficulties on the attempt to publish *Beyond the Pale* and attacks the book 'as part of a combined and planned effort to harass the ICN', and sees it as 'a debasement of Christian moral standards'.

That the ICN has failed to reach even modest targets in three years is clear from an appeal mailed in September 1981 which re-affirms the now desperate financial plight of the Network, its inability to meet its obligations to its Executive Secretary or to continue its work without very substantial donations. The sum of £14,000 is named just to stay afloat.

More revelations

Far more damaging to the 'integrity' of secret collaborators of the DOI round the world will be the publication of books by Dr Eschel Rhoodie and by Gordon Winter. Gordon Winter is a self-confessed agent of BOSS – the South African Bureau of State Security, now living quietly in Ireland. His book *Inside BOSS*, due from Allen Lane in the autumn of 1981, will take the lid off various South African 'dirty tricks' in Europe.

Winter first went to South Africa in 1960 and got a job as crime reporter on the Johannesburg *Sunday Express*. In an interview on television in 1979 he said that the country was good to him and he wanted to do something in return. He became a spy. He was deported from South Africa in somewhat mysterious circumstances and worked as a freelance journalist, which work included assignments for Forum World Features. He specialized in stories about South African exiles and attended many anti-apartheid meetings.

As part of his journalistic work he became membership secretary of the National Union of Journalists' London freelance branch and as a result had access to the files and address list of well known opponents of apartheid.

One of Winter's tasks was to discredit such people and especially the Liberal Party whose members at the time (1969/70) were dramatically involved in the boycott of sporting links with South Africa and other anti-apartheid campaigns. It was Winter who in 1971 somehow got hold of the story about Jeremy Thorpe's relationship with Norman Scott and tried, unsuccessfully, to sell it to Fleet Street. The South African covert operation against the Liberals intensified during the run up to the 1974 election. There were suspicions that the arrest of Peter Hain for an alleged bank robbery was an attempted frame-up to undermine the work of the Young Liberals.

Gordon Winter returned to South Africa the day before the 1974 British General Election. The circumstances were as strange as those surrounding his deportation from that country in 1960s. For a time he worked again on the Johannesburg *Sunday Express* and then left to join *The Citizen*, the paper created and funded covertly by the Department of Information.

In the wake of Muldergate, he fled South Africa and went into hiding. In a television interview on London Weekend TV on 29 June 1979 he told part of his story and hinted at more to come.

Another element of the anti-Liberal campaign was a broadsheet called *The Hidden Face of the Liberal Party* which was widely distributed in constituencies where the Liberals were strongly represented. This broadsheet was published by Geoffrey Stewart-Smith's Foreign Affairs Publishing Co (see Footnote in Chapter 2).

Part of Winter's book will inevitably deal with aspects of his working with his South African 'handler' General Jacobus Kemp. One particular episode was widely reported in the South African press in December 1980. It concerned the attempted cover-up of the real nature of the Club of Ten. The Club of Ten was a clandestine body which controlled and financed an international advertising propaganda campaign to sell apartheid to the European and North American public through the purchase of space in the most respected newspapers. It cost over R400,000 during its three years of operation.

During an early stage of the Muldergate investigations in September 1978, when General Kemp was himself heading a committee assigned to enquire into the information scandal, he seems to have decided to divert attention away from the DOI by arranging a 'secret' meeting of the rich South African businessmen who were supposedly behind the Club and who gave it its name. At the same time the meeting place in a Johannesburg hotel would be leaked to the press by Gordon Winter so that the Club could be 'caught' at a legitimate meeting without any Information Department influence. Winter who was working for *The Citizen*, a DOI sponsored newspaper, was unable, for obvious reasons, to make the leak himself, so he arranged for his girlfriend to 'leak' the story to the *Star*. The plot failed because no journalist discovered the 'meeting' and the face-saving press story fed to the papers later in the night convinced no one.

In London the Club of Ten had Suite 66 at 87 Regent Street. At Suite 63 was the National Association for Freedom. In the winter of 1976/77 John Gouriet, NAF's Director challenged, in the courts, a boycott of the South African regime by the British Postal Workers Union. On 8 February 1977, in the midst of this controversy, the Club of Ten, placed a quarter-page advertisement in the London *Daily Telegraph* which challenged Tom Jackson, the Secretary of the Postal Workers Union, to announce a boycott of postal and telegraphic services to the Soviet Union, East Germany and Angola.

Another project is listed as G26P. There is on the face of it, no such organisation in London but there are several which could possibly fit the general description and only a few which have close South African links. Perhaps the expected Rhoodie book called *The Great Information Scandal* will shed some light on the remaining mysteries in the secret project list, but the delay in the publication of the much-heralded work makes one wonder whether the South African Government may not have done a deal with Dr Rhoodie to suppress the inconvenient secrets in his head, in return for freedom from further harassment.

Revenge for exposing Muldergate

While Dr Rhoodie's Grand Design to buy influence aboard has been challenged, exposed and halted, it does not mean that all the projects have ceased. Now however, it is much more difficult in South Africa to investigate cases and publish findings. So many doors have been slammed shut and locked.

Dr Rhoodie's plan included the buying of newspapers, magazines, newsletters so that they could be used to promote Nationalist Party news and views or at least reflect an approving attitude. When the efforts to purchase suitable journals in Britain, France, the United States and within South Africa itself failed, or were exposed, the South African Government tried another manoeuvre. It tried to restrict still further the freedom of the press and other news media within the country itself. The SABC has a monopoly over all

South African radio and TV broadcasting and has always been subject to political manipulation. It has propagated a narrow Nationalist view of African affairs and has never deviated from its support of South Africa as a bastion of white Christian civilisation. In 1980 a number of producers who showed even faint signs of independent thinking were arbitrarily dismissed.

The government appointed the Steyn Commission to investigate and report on press handling of security matters. Its recommendations, not surprisingly, were a further threat to press freedom. A national communications policy was suggested as part of the 'national strategy'. In other words, the press should reflect the needs of the white regime. There was to be less negative reporting – in other words, less investigations of official corruption or scandal. Finally Steyn recommended restrictions on press reporting of terrorist activities, especially seeking to ban reporting on terrorist goals or demands. Given the wide definition of terrorism in South Africa to include almost all democratic forms of protest as well as violent groups, this was seen by the black community as just another way of silencing black aspirations.

It is difficult to take a charitable view of such recommendations in the face of the activities described in this book or in the teeth of South African Government attempts to conceal the extent of South African armed intervention in the Angolan civil war and covert military support of UNITA, a discredited guerrilla force which once received support of the CIA and now relies on professional mercenaries.

In the closing months of 1980, the South African authorities banned the *Post* and *Sunday Post*, two newspapers with wide circulation in the black community, 'denying black people' as the acting editor of the *Post* said, 'the basic right to be informed of what is happening around them'. The Minister of Justice had alleged that the two newspapers, owned by a large white-controlled newspaper group, were aimed at creating a revolutionary climate in South Africa. It was a charge as absurd as accusing *The People* and *The Sun* in Britain of fomenting revolution.

The South African Prime Minister's earlier public reassurances of his determination to propose and implement meaningful changes in the system of apartheid have proved to be false – repressive legislation, intimidation of labour and large-scale evictions of squatters, forced transportations to the homelands hit only the blacks.

The government has made it abundantly clear that it does not wish the black community to have a public voice. Severe banning orders were served on two prominent and distinguished black journalists Mr Zwelakhe Sisulu, news editor of the *Sunday Post*, and Mr Marimuthu Subramoney from Durban. Both were senior officials of the growing Media Workers' Association of South Africa (MWASA), a black trade union which was slowly and carefully improving conditions for black workers in publishing, formalising training and improved recruiting schemes for young blacks. The bannings evoked widespread protest at home and abroad. Ken Ashton, the General Secretary of the National Union of Journalists who flew into Johannesburg to meet black journalists, was refused admittance and put on the next plane to London. Len Murray of the Trades Unions Congress commented that 'the action of the South African regime fits into a familiar pattern of action to harass and intimidate black working people who are making great strides in developing the independent trade union organisations through which they can improve their employment conditions and break down the unacceptable disparities arising from the application of the hateful policy of apartheid'.

Bishop Desmond Tutu, himself the victim of a sordid campaign of character assassination and threat of violence, had recently had his passport seized for the second time by the authorities to prevent his travel abroad when he addressed the first annual congress of the Southern Transvaal region of MWASA in February 1981 in Soweto. It had become an occupational hazard to be a journalist in South Africa, he said. It was even more of risk if you were a black journalist. Five black MWASA members had been detained in recent months.

'I'm optimistic that we are going to attain freedom in South Africa in five years' the bishop said, 'but the cost is going to be horrendous. The struggle is going to be costly.'

'Many are still going to be detained, banned, harassed and some are still going to be shot in the streets.'

172

'Even when we say that we are striving and committed toward peaceful change we are regarded as the enemy. Even when our people are engaged in peaceful demonstrations they are still regarded as the enemy.'

Characteristically Tutu challenged both black and white communities. To black journalists he said 'You have to decide whether you are going to soft pedal and survive or risk this new occupational hazard. You are now clearly in the frontline.' To the white population he said 'Whites must use the period between now and when we have genuine democratic government for making friends with blacks. There is yet goodwill left.'

This goodwill is stressed in strong terms in every issue of *The Voice*. *The Voice* is the only black owned newspaper in the whole of South Africa and it is published under the protecting arm of the South African Council of Churches. It started after the Soweto riots of 1976 and now has a circulation of some 35,000 copies. It reflects at least in part, the authentic feelings of the black community and provides a platform for black intellectuals.

Despite its moderate content, *The Voice* has proved such a thorn in the government flesh that it was banned 26 times in 1978. It overturned on appeal a 27th and final ban and has continued to publish ever since. It has now added the words 'of the voiceless' to its logo. The board of management includes most of South Africa's key black religious leaders representing many churches and denominations. It is subsidised by grants from churches overseas and from the World Council of Churches. In the tense atmosphere of South Africa, *The Voice* provides a serious medium for international and domestic news and features of concern to the black community. As pressure on press freedom increases it becomes increasingly important.

In June 1981, journalists felt themselves further threatened by the sudden dismissal of Alistair Sparks, the crusading editor of the *Rand Daily Mail*, after 22 years with the newspaper. The management gave as a reason the paper's poor profit record. The government however has sought ways of getting rid of Mr Sparks for many years, and cynics have seen him as a sacrificial lamb offered up to prevent further government action against the press as a result of recommendations from the Steyn Commission. Whatever the causes, most commentators were convinced that the removal of Mr Sparks and his replacement by an Afrikaans would have serious journalistic and political consequences in South Africa. The black community who saw one of their champions dismissed would wonder why. It was the *Mail* which led the press in uncovering the Information scandal and in doing so changed the course South African history. Was the dismissal a sort of revenge?

Alistair Sparks, in his valedictory address, borrowed the words of William Randolph Hearst, the American newspaper tycoon, to describe the *Rand Daily Mail* as having comforted the afflicted and afflicted the comfortable in a society where the differences between the two are probably greater than anywhere. The same conjunction of ideas applies equally well to the South African Council of Churches. The English-speaking press and the churches have been important centres of moral resistance to the policies of apartheid and to the insolence of white privilege. Neither have been able to prevent the harassment of innocent black communities, the forced removals of squatters, the migratory labour system, the bannings and imprisonments or the inhuman strategy of the homelands. Nor have they been able to interrupt the growth of military power or halt its provocative acts of aggression in neighbouring countries. They have, however, given the widest publicity to each violation, deplored each broken political promise, offered constructive alternatives for peaceful change. All this despite blundering and violent attempts to destroy their authority.

Supporters of the South African political system always point to the double standards of their most vociferous critics. They maintain that the Soviet Union has a worse record of atrocities and repression than South Africa. They may well be true but protest on behalf of the victims of oppression in the Soviet Union can seldom be more than a volley of words. South Africa is a different matter. It calls itself a Christian country and its problems are rooted in the recent history and political policies of Britain and of the rich industrialised nations. There are ties of investment, trade, history and of blood. All of these provide opportunities of leverage and influence. Where money speaks loudest, in the fields of international trade, of banking and finance and of the sharing of military information and expertise, leverage to accelerate change has scarcely been applied. By labelling any challenge directed at breaking economic links between South Africa and the rich nations as Communist inspired, the work of the enemy, South Africa and its supporters have won time, but it is time which will be paid for in spilled blood and ironically in the growth of influence of those very forces it is supposed to roll back.

South Africa – a new ally for President Reagan?

When Ronald Reagan became President of the United States a new policy towards South Africa was inevitable. Relationships had been cool at the official level during the administration of Mr Carter. His policies had been supportive of official United Nations moves to isolate South Africa until real changes in the apartheid system were implemented. Large-scale investment was discouraged. Military assistance was outlawed. Mr Reagan and his new team wanted to be friends and to sweep away as much of the restriction of the previous presidency as possible. Washington was no longer deaf to Pretoria.

As far as the promotion of South African policies in the States was concerned, it was no longer necessary to operate the covert type of propaganda projects organised during the time of Dr Rhoodie. Donald de Kieffer, South Africa's lobbyist in Washington at the height of the Information campaign was part of Mr Reagan's transition team and then was rewarded with a post as general counsel to Special Trade Representative Bill Brock. This was described in the Richmond-Times Despatch of 17 May 1981 as 'another illustration of the new love affair of the Reagan administration with South Africa.'

New public affairs consultants were hired. John P Sears of the law firm of Baskin and Sears and Ronald Reagan's former campaign manager, was hired at 500,000 US dollars a year. The firm of Smathers, Symington and Herlong of Washington was also retained at 300,000 US dollars a year and expenses. These expenses in 1980 included generous gifts to selected congressmen and senators seeking election, the details of which are revealed in statements filed with the Department of Justice under Section 2 of the Foreign Agents Registration Act of 1938, as amended.

The United States representative on the UN Security Council at the first opportunity vetoed an attempt to declare a trade embargo against South Africa because of its policy in Namibia. The new administration favoured investment; human rights considerations scarcely mattered.

Another of the secret projects initiated by Dr Rhoodie centred around John McGoff and the Panax newspaper group. Sworn evidence given to the Erasmus Commission investigating the DOI slush fund projects in South Africa indicated that McGoff was the key to a large-scale propaganda exercise in the United States (see Chapter Five) with the help of funds made available through a Swiss subsidiary of the Union Bank, called Thesaurus Continental Securities. This company was set up specifically as a front organisation for South Africa's BOSS. The Erasmus Commission revealed that at least 11,750,000 US dollars was passed to McGoff to help buy a national newspaper, the *Washington Star* and a TV news agency UPITN on behalf of the South Africans. Neither deal succeeded. Thesaurus also owned a large seaside villa at Miami Beach which McGoff apparently used and claimed as his own.[2]

The evidence offered to Erasmus alerted the US media and the government security watchdogs that it was possible for a foreign country to buy controlling interests in influential papers in the States through which it could manipulate public opinion. The constitutional safeguards were not enough. A federal investigation of McGoff was begun to see whether and how he might have violated federal law acting as an unregistered agent of the South African government. With Ronald Reagan at the White House, it seems as if the grand jury investigation has lost impetus and it is doubtful now whether it will ever report.

The New Right and its Christian allies

Two separate but unrelated streams of thought have profoundly altered the American political landscape in the last year or so and are partly responsible for the success of

---

[2] Karen Rothmyer. The McGoff Grab. Columbia Journalism Review. Nov/Dec 1979.

President Reagan. The first is the development of a far-reaching network of well-financed think tanks and research organisations which are able to produce, as one commentator has put it, a paper avalanche of conservative thinking on all kinds of political and social issues. On foreign policy, for example, it is a publicly acknowledged fact that Ronald Reagan was a regular participant in seminars at the Hoover Institution on War, Revolution and Peace, throughout the run-up period to his final election campaign. Richard V Allen, a former Hoover Institution academic, co-ordinated Reagan's foreign policy statements. He is a strong advocate of increased spending on defence.

The Hoover Institution was the brainchild of President Herbert Hoover in 1919. Its charter commands it 'to demonstrate the evils of the doctrines of Karl Marx – whether communism, socialism, economic materialism, or atheism – thus to protect the American way of life from such ideologies their conspiracies, and to reaffirm the validity of the American system'. Such an extreme position exposed the Institution to ridicule and contempt during the period of more liberal politics of the sixties and early seventies but the centre of gravity has shifted sharply to the right and Hoover and many similar organisations form a network which is now in the mainstream of political thinking. Money and good public relations have been part of their success. The source of the money is not the foundations which are household names for social and liberal programmes – the Ford and the Rockefeller Foundations for instance. It comes from another generation of millionaires and businessmen, Coors, Noble, Scaife, Richardson and others.

Richard Mellon Scaife, for instance, has already appeared in this book (see Chapter Five). He was briefly linked with John McGoff in the purchase of a Californian-based group of newspapers. In 1973, he became the owner of Kern House Enterprises, the American company which owned Forum World Features in London which was CIA-owned and funded in earlier years without the knowledge of many of the journalists who worked for it, as 'a significant means to counter Communist propaganda'. Scaife is one of the wealthiest Americans at the present time. He is not only the second largest shareholder in the Mellon Bank, one of the top twenty banks in the United States, but he receives an income running into many millions from two trusts set up for him by his mother. He controls the income from many of the family trusts and foundations which together have assets in excess of 250 million US dollars. In 1957 when Fortune Magazine tried to rank the largest fortunes in America, four Mellons, including Scaife's mother, Sarah Mellon Scaife, were amongst the top eight.

According to Karen Rothmyer, a former Wall Street reporter, in a long and carefully researched feature in *Columbia Journalism Review* July/August 1981, Scaife in the seventies became part of the powerful new political movement which was to culminate in the election of Ronald Reagan – the New Right. He and the family trusts he controlled or influenced became one of the biggest backers of conservative causes. 'Ten years ago' reported the *Washington Post* on 4 January 1981, 'the Sarah Mellon Scaife Foundation in Pittsburgh with assets of 100 million US dollars, gave mainly to traditional community causes such as the opera and the United Negro College Fund. Today its list of 'public affairs' recipients reads like a Who's Who of the conservative network, a shift reflecting the interests of Richard Mellon Scaife, the foundation's chairman and a Republican campaign contributor.'

'Institute for Contemporary Studies, Hoover, Georgetown; Center for Strategic and International Studies, Mid-America; Legal Foundation; Institute for Research on the Economics of Taxation; Freedoms Foundation; Center for Entrepreneurial Development; Council for Basic Education; Ethics and Public Policy Center; Law and Economic Center for the Study of American Business'. The Heritage Foundation, a conservative think tank that supplied eleven members of the Reagan transition team acknowledge that Scaife is a far bigger contributor than Joseph Coors, whose name has been the only one mentioned in most press reports on the group.

Military and intelligence think tanks and academic programmes are particularly favoured by Scaife. The National Strategy Information Center is one of them. The Institute for the Study of Conflict in London is another.

The NSIC, FARI, Aims, together with the Thyssen Foundation of West Germany, the Center for International and Strategic Studies of Indonesia and the Comitato Atlantico

Italiano sponsored a conference at Brighton in June 1978. An important guest was Richard Mellon Scaife. Another American guest was William J Casey, the man who was to be Reagan's choice as new Director of the CIA in 1981. There was a carefully selected cross-section of guests from South Africa, the NATO countries and from Asia. 'Men who may not be conspicuously cited by history, but yet have a hand in shaping it in quiet and selfless ways . . . individuals who belong to powerful groups, political parties, and influential institutes . . . (who) have the capacity, therefore, to transmit ideas to very large constituencies', as Frank Barnett, President of NSIC and Board member of the Washington Institute for the Study of Conflict said in his opening address.

One of the main subjects of the Brighton conference was a plan to set up a world anti-communist organisation to be financed by private companies or foundations. The strong participation of the South Africans whose government had backed at least one of the conference sponsoring bodies was aimed at influencing NATO military personnel and governments to stand by South Africa and harden their line towards the Soviet Union to fill the gap created by the American military and moral retreat from the world arena in the wake of Watergate and Vietnam. In an attempt to make the occasion an historic one, the conference issued The Brighton Declaration, which stated: 'The destruction of the CIA and other assaults on Western intelligence sources make it imperative that the US and its allies should again take the initiative on intelligence, information and counter-intelligence'. The draft of the declaration was prepared by Brian Crozier, the then Director of the Institute for the Study of Conflict. Crozier, a former journalist and director of Forum World Features until it closed in 1975 was well-known as a person of extreme right-wing views. His book, *Strategy of Survival,** echoes the concern of Brighton. 'By 1975' he says, 'the CIA had been virtually destroyed as an instrument for the execution of American foreign policy . . . the blocking of CIA funds destined to help non-Marxist nationalist movements in Angola was a disaster.' All of this he argued was evidence of 'the decline of the American will'. Elsewhere he looks forward to a time when under a new President and Administration, untainted by Watergate, the CIA can be restored. 'Secret intelligence operations' he maintains, 'far surpass military ones in certain circumstances.'

From 1973 onwards the American NSIC helped finance the ISC in London. It supplied money and expertise to enable the ISC to publish its Annual of Power and Conflict and maintain a living Index of Extremist Movements. In some years at least the NSIC was covering the salary of a research assistant plus advertising and printing costs of the Annual. At all times it offered a valuable sales outlet in the States for the books. NSIC is linked to the Committee on the Present Danger (CPD) a group which has opposed SALT II and supports a strongly interventionist US foreign policy. CPD is also supported by Scaife grants. All these groups now play a major part in the shape of American politics and have their allies in Britain. The growth of a parallel intelligence network with a cold war theme, the sharing of mailings, publications, black-lists of 'tainted' organisations or individuals, ties to private security services with huge financial sources to spy, to create propagada and in some cases to terrorise, is a possible and logical outcome of such fraternal interchanges. They may, indeed, most do, function within the legal limits imposed by their registered aims and objectives but there are dangers here which need to be guarded against. The most prestigious think tanks have a 'guru' status which gives them phenomenal influence. Why shouldn't some rich millionaire with a vision give huge grants to institutions which can apply political leverage to influence the course of history?

The second development which is shaping political opinion in the United States is the growth of a new religious lobbying force – the Christian allies of the political New Right. Two of the groups, Christian Voice and Moral Majority, are registered as non-profit, non-exempt bodies and can therefore lobby as extensively as they wish and even take part in election campaigns.

The new groups have their roots in Protestant fundamentalist and evangelical churches. They are backed by prominent television preachers and have links with New Right political organisations as well as old-style conservative members of Congress. They have huge followings, huge financial resources, highly committed leadership and organisation. They

* Strategy of Survival. pub. Temple Smith. London, 1978.

176

have declared war on immorality in American society, on 'secular humanism' in the schools and elsewhere, and on government interference in Christian education and other church concerns. They act with old-fashioned missionary zeal and they are intolerant of any swerving from their perceived path of righteousness.

Christian Voice was founded in 1978 by a Californian travel agent Robert Gordon Grant who had served as an assistant pastor of eight years with W S McBirnie of Glendale Community Church and other church organisations (see Chapter 7 for his involvement with Rev Fred Shaw and Christian League of Southern Africa). In its first year it recruited, according to US News and World Report 24 September 1979, 126,000 members – including nearly 1,200 Protestant ministers and 300 Roman Catholic priests. 16 members of Congress had joined its advisory committee and it had budgetted 3 million US dollars for political lobbying for the 1980 election, some of which would be donated towards the election funds of conservative candidates who met the specifications of the Voice's 'morality scale'. This scale was based on how candidates stood on such issues as homosexuality, pornography, government spending, defence and sanctions against (at that time) Mr Smith's Zimbabwe/Rhodesia, SALT II, recognition of the Peoples Republic of China, capital punishment.

One of Christian Voice's first major campaigns was to try and lift US economic sanctions against Rhodesia. It circulated a leaflet similar in style and content to those of the CLSA together with letters from Iowa senator Roger Jepsen and P K F V van der Byl, the then foreign minister of Rhodesia, and Robert Grant, Voice's President. 'Your gift decides the life or death of a Christian nation' Grant's letter said. 'Think about the innocent children being shot to death because they love Jesus' Jepson's letter warned that 'the media' might mislead Christians about the issues involved in Rhodesia's attempt to establish a biracial government.

Its direct mailing fund raising campaign is organised by Jerry Hunsinger, a former Methodist minister of Richmond Virginia whose accounts include the television preachers Jerry Falwell and Robert Schuller, the singer Anita Bryant's anti-gay and profamily work, Citizens for Decency through Law. He also supervises fund raising for the Moral Majority. A democratic Congressional Campaign Committee Report compiled in March 1980 warned that Christian Voice was reaching some 40 million Christian viewers through existing Christian Television networks using commercials designed to motivate the viewer to take action on current issues. It planned to generate up to a quarter of a million letters, postcards or telegrams to Congress on any given issue. Such a demonstration of public opinion was calculated to have a strong influence on any legislation before Congress.

The Moral Majority movement was founded by a TV evangelist from Lychburg, Virginia. It now has branches in 46 states and a newsletter that reaches 248,000 people, including 70,000 conservative pastors. The Moral Majority has a similar programme to Christian Voice, but Falwell also puts emphasis on the rejection of the equal-rights amendment (ERA), which he has called 'a vicious attack on the monogamous Christian home'.

Another popular television evangelist is Pat Robertson whose Christian Broadcasting Network has a viewership of some 7 million and an income from donations of over 50 million dollars and rising. Far more money, as one journalist points out, than any presidential candidate has for his campaign. Robertson personally endorsed his own chosen congressional candidates and gave air-time to several well-known conservative congressmen including Larry McDonald, a leader of the John Birch Society, who argued for the cancellation of many of the federal social programmes because they were unconstitutional. Robertson hosted Ian Smith, the Rhodesian premier on his 700 Club programme and personally sermonised against the WCC for 'purchasing guns for revolutionaries'.

At the same time as this growth of conservative Christian activity, it appears that the influence of the so-called mainline denominations – Methodists, Presbyterians, Episcopalians – who backed liberal anti-war and civil rights campaigns in the sixties, has declined. For decades these churches have been trying to move the evangelicals towards a reasonable discussion of the need for commitment on political issues and have been taken very much by surprise at the direction in which they have bolted.

What was once a barely visible Christian political fringe has now come to the centre of the stage and with the help of the backers of the New Right is taking on the dimensions of a global campaign. It is difficult to see whether this is a passing phenomenon or a permanent feature of the world scene.

The large-scale clandestine campaign orchestrated by Dr Rhoodie on behalf of the white South African regime has ceased and many of the supportive groups and individuals who jumped on the bandwagon have jumped off again. What remains is a sense of bewilderment, of let-down and pent-up energy with nowhere to go.

At the same time support for the work of the World Council of Churches has grown and the public debate which continues challenges Christians and others to look at the issues.

In this 'postscript' to the postscript the author wishes to share with his readers a press report in the American and British press during the third week of September 1981 which shows that even under President Reagan's supportive presidency, the New Right and its Christian allies are not having it all their own way. After three days of polite but searching questioning by a Senate panel, reported the *Christian Science Monitor*, 'the message rang clear that all the fury of the right-to-lifers (anti-abortionists) cannot stop Sandra Day O'Connor from becoming the first woman to sit in the nation's highest court.

The caucus of extreme right-wingers was headed on the one hand by Senator Jesse Helms about whom even American conservatives agree that if he moved further right he would drop off the edge, and the Rev Carl McIntyre, the veteran fundamentalist radio preacher, whose life long crusade against all movement towards Christian unity had been discussed (see index for page references).

To Senator Helms, Ms O'Connor displayed dangerously liberal tendencies, and he feared she would not prove an ally in efforts to overturn what he regards as permissive legislation, but in the hearing she came over as a conscientious, fair-minded conservative and she refused to give her legal opinions on specific issues – such as bussing or abortion – which excited the extremists. It was clear that she would give no comfort to the New Right. In the end the Rev Carl McIntyre was left glaring at the chairman Strom Thurmond and protesting 'I think this thing's been stacked'.

The Senate went on to confirm the appointment of Ms O'Connor to the Supreme Court by a margin of 99 to nil, the largest margin ever recorded.

Appendix 1
Useful Contacts and Addresses in the United Kingdom

AFFOR, 1 Finch Road, Lozells, Birmingham B19 1HS. AFFOR stands for All Faiths for One Race. An organization financed by charitable trusts concerned with racial harmony. It publishes pamphlets etc, and engages in educational work in schools and elsewhere.

Board of Deputies of British Jews, Woburn House, Upper Woburn Place, London WC1H 0EP. It has an information service covering all kinds of contemporary political and religious movements, in particular those engaged in anti-semitic or other racist activity. It publishes reports and a news-letter *The Defender* — 'in defence of racial and religious harmony in Britain'.

CARAF (Christians Against Racism and Fascism) 1 Finch Road, Lozells, Birmingham B19 1HS. A loose grouping of representatives of Christian organizations making a Christian response to the growth of racism and fascism in Britain. Events, rallies and newsheets.

Catholic Institute for International Relations, 1 Cambridge Terrace, Regents Park, London NW1; a campaigning Catholic agency specializing in Latin America, Southern Africa and the Yemen; expert and authoritative publications on political, social and economic aspects of Zimbabwe (Rhodesia).

Community and Race Relations Unit (CRRU), British Council of Churches, 2 Eaton Gate, London SW1 9BL. Publications, reading lists, quarterly newsletter suitable for church and other groups; organizes seminars, supports projects in the UK. Bookshop of BCC and WCC publications at above address.

Counter-Information Services, 9 Poland Street, London W1; financed by charitable trusts and by churches to publish information not collected or covered by the established media; has published several reports on South Africa and on the role of multinationals.

Christian Aid, 240 Ferndale Road, London SW9 8BH. An agency of the British Council of Churches whose mandate is to relieve or combat mal-nutrition, hunger, sickness and distress throughout the world. Publications and educational materials available.

Defence and Aid Fund of Southern Africa, 104 Newgate Street, London EC1. A humanitarian organization working for peaceful and constructive solutions to the problems caused by racial oppression in southern Africa; comprehensive information service, publications and newsletters.

State Research, 9 Poland Street, London W1; an independent group of investigators collecting and publishing information from public sources on developments in state policy, in particular the law, internal security, espionage and the military, the right and paramilitary organizations.

Appendix 2
Select Bibliography

A Briefing on the Right Wing; an Analytical Compilation of Resources, by Peggy Ann Lou Shriver, for the Office of Research, National Council of Churches, New York. Booklet surveying trends and organizations active up to 1978 in the United States.

Catholicism and World Order, by Professor Michael Dummett. Pub CIIR. Acute reflections on the 1978 Reith Lectures by Dr Norman (35p).

Christianity and Race in Britain Today, by John Hick, Professor of Theology at Birmingham University, published by AFFOR, booklet. The problem in a nutshell, compassionate and clearly written (15p).

Christians or Capitalists?, by Cosmas Desmond, Bowerdean Press, 1978. Christianity and politics in South Africa. Vigorous arguments on behalf of a 'church of the oppressed'.

A Christian Looks at the National Front, by Malcolm Goldsmith, available from CRRU (see useful addresses). The background of the NF written to help Christians understand what was happening in 1977. It is dated now but has good insights (30p).

Christians, Politics and Violent Revolution, by Gordon Davies, SCM Press, 1976. An English theologian assembles the many strands of liberation theology and explains them sympathetically. Essential reading for those who want to understand the contemporary search for a 'popular' church.

Fascists, by Michael Billig, Harcourt Brace Jovanovich, 1978. A social psychological view of the NF in the form of a scholarly discussion of the underlying ideology and structures of modern fascism.

Information Pack on the National Front, prepared by Dr Jacob Gewirtz for the Board of Deputies of British Jews. Published April 1979 to provide information useful during the election. A collection of materials, quotations, booklets, including *They Stand Condemned – what every Christian should know about the National Front*, by the Bishops of Southwark and Woolwich. Most helpful.

Race Propaganda and South Africa, by John C Laurence, Victor Gollancz, 1979 (£6.95). An exposé of the manipulation of Western opinion and policies by the South African white nationalists. Written from the inside, it is an analysis of the propaganda and reality of apartheid. Well documented. Written before Muldergate.

The Great White Hoax, Africa Bureau, London, 1977. A critical survey of South African propaganda tactics at home and abroad.

The National Front: Racialism and neo-Fascism in Britain, by Peter

Shipley. A Conflict Studies pamphlet for the Institute for the Study of Conflict, 1978 (£2). An objective political analysis containing useful information.

Searchlight, A F and R Publications, 21 Great Western Buildings, 6 Livery Street, Birmingham 3 (30p). A monthly anti-fascist magazine; investigative journalism of personalities and events and connections of the right.

Southern Africa. A study pack for British Christians about South Africa, Namibia and Zimbabwe, and our Christian response. Available from Christian Aid, Cafod or CIIR, 1979, (£3). Fact sheets, background leaflets, Bible studies etc.

Terrorism and the Liberal State, by Paul Wilkinson, Macmillans, 1977 (£2.95). It examines the problem of terrorism in the modern world and the very real dilemmas that we all have to think about.

Shalom and Combat, by Albert van den Heuvel, World Council of Churches (£2.25). A personal struggle against racism by a distinguished Dutch Christian with a lifetime of working in the ecumenical movement.

Race: No Peace without Justice, by Barbara Rogers, World Council of Churches, 1981 (£2.50). The WCC's consultations on racism, set in the context of the whole debate within the churches.

Appendix 3
Select List of Underground Newspapers and Broadsheets

Only those mentioned in the text are included.

British Gazette	100 Philbeach Gardens, London SW5. Dowager Lady Jane Birdwood's paper for The Self Help and Current Affairs Association whose aim is to campaign against union 'tyranny'.
Bulldog	Young National Front, 91 Connaught Road, Teddington, Middlesex. Official youth paper of NF.
Choice	100 Philbeach Gardens, London SW5. Dowager Lady Jane Birdwood's newspaper format broadsheet for the Anti-Immigration Standing Committee.
East-West Digest	Foreign Affairs Publishing Co, Church House, Petersham Road, Richmond, Surrey. Monthly (temporarily suspended) strongly anti-communist, pro-apartheid news on world security.
Gateway	Gate House, 27 Middleton Road, Brentwood, Essex. Bernard Simmons' religious magazine sympathetic to CAC and CLSA material.
League Review	13 Langdon Court, City Road, London EC1. Published on behalf of the League of St George.
Liverpool Newsletter	c/o Anthony Cooney, Rose Cottage, 17 Hadassah Grove, Park Lane, Liverpool L17 8XH. An occasional broadsheet in support of Social Credit, the NF and the British Movement
The National Message	British Israel World Federation, 6 Buckingham Gate, London SW1. A monthly magazine with photos. Official journal of BIWF.
New Tomorrow	The Holy Spirit Association for the Unification of World Christianity, 3 Barn Hill, Wembley, Middlesex. Popularly known as The Moonies. Monthly glossy magazine. See also One World.
One World	Ditto, weekly broadsheet.
On Target	Intelligence Publications (UK), The Old Priory, Priory Walk, Sudbury, Suffolk. Donald Martin's fortnightly newsheet, anti-EEC, anti-communist, anti-immigration, generally pro-apartheid.

Appendix 3: underground newspapers and broadsheets

Open Eye c/o Bernard Smith (Christian Affirmation Campaign), 124 Heath Park Road, Gidea Park, Essex. Occasional newsletter of the CAC; small circulation; editor writes it is about 'subversion of the Christian faith by Marxist Politics'.

Race and Nation c/o Edgar Bullen, 35 Hollingbury Road, Brighton, Sussex. Published by the Racial Preservation Society which is anti-immigration, anti-semitic, politically extremist.

Salvo 303 Cauldwell Hall Road, Ipswich IP4 5AJ. Anti-Marxist, supportive of British Movement, quarterly. First issue carried big extract from *The Fraudulent Gospel*. Now merged with *Valkyrie*.

Spearhead Seacroft, 52 Westbourne Villas, Hove, Sussex. Monthly magazine published by John Tyndall for the National Front.

Truth and Liberty c/o David Scoffins, 38 Meadow Road, Royston, Barnsley, Yorkshire S71 4AJ. Home-made roneo broadsheet. No 1 only so far. Off-prints CAC material — racist, anti-WCC etc.

Ulster Sentinel PO Box 3, Newtownabbey, County Antrim, Ulster. Anti-WCC, sectarian.

Valkyrie A Hampson Services, 303 Cauldwell Hall Road, Ipswich IP4 5AJ. Quarterly bulletin describing itself as organ of The Phoenix Society — an Odinist group and breakaway from the Anglo-Saxonic Church.

Wake Up! British Israel World Federation, 6 Buckingham Gate, London SW1. A monthly glossy magazine for the BIWF; photos etc.

183

Appendix 4
Distribution Pattern of TFG

UK Publisher	Foreign Affairs Publishing Co, Church House, Petersham Road, Richmond, Surrey. 2nd edition in 1979.
South African Publisher	Valiant Publishers
American Publisher	Church League of America, 422 North Prospect Street, Wheaton, Illinois 60187.

Sold in the UK by:

Alternative Bookshop, 40 Floral Street, London WC2. Announced itself as a 'right-wing bookshop' — alternative to Collets etc.

Augustine Publishing Co, South View, Chawleigh, Chulmleigh, Devon EX18 7HL. A mail order company run by a Catholic traditionalist Timothy Tindal-Robertson who bought up The Britons Publishing Co and archive; mainly devotional literature but also includes a general list of 'conspiracy literature' etc.

Bloomfield Books, The Old Priory, Priory Walk, Sudbury, Suffolk. A mail order catalogue acting as outlet for Donald Martin's British League of Rights and other fronts. List includes racist and conspiracy literature.

Covenant Publishing Co, 6 Buckingham Gate, London SW1. The bookshop of the British Israel World Federation: works as a charity. 'Political' books for sale 'under the counter'.

A Hampson Services, 303 Cauldwell Hall Road, Ipswich IP4 5AJ. Small shop, mainly mail order suppliers, militaria, political and religious books: closely connected to the British Movement.

KRP Publications Ltd, 245 Cann Hall Road, London E11. A mail order catalogue of Social Credit and mainly imported 'conspiracy' literature — similar to Bloomfield Books.

Nationalist Bookshop, Excalibur House, 73 Great Eastern Street, London EC2A 3HU. The National Front's bookshop.

Pro Fide Book Service -- see St Duthac's Book Service.

St Duthac's Book Service, 39 Blenheim Park Road, South Croydon. A Catholic mail order list, mainly devotional but sympathetic to Tridentine Mass plus a short collection of religio-political works.

Sunwheel Distributors, PO Box 19, Hayes, Middlesex. A mail order catalogue of selected extremist political, racist, anti-semitic and conspiracy literature: similar to Historical Review Press. Racial Preservation Society, Northern League sympathies.

Tancoed Publications, c/o A H Underwood, 3 Minclywd, Melin-y-Wig, Corwen, LL21 9RL, North Wales. Similar list to Military World — A Hampson Services. Mail order, militaria and militant literature: a British Movement front.

Index

Index

Index

190

Index